Cambridge Elements

Elements in Gender and Politics
edited by
Tiffany D. Barnes
University of Texas at Austin
Diana Z. O'Brien
Washington University in St. Louis

PUBLIC PREFERENCES, GENDER, AND FOREIGN SUPPORT FOR ARMED MOVEMENTS

Çağlayan Başer
Bilkent University

Shaftesbury Road, Cambridge CB2 8EA, United Kingdom

One Liberty Plaza, 20th Floor, New York, NY 10006, USA

477 Williamstown Road, Port Melbourne, VIC 3207, Australia

314–321, 3rd Floor, Plot 3, Splendor Forum, Jasola District Centre,
New Delhi – 110025, India

103 Penang Road, #05-06/07, Visioncrest Commercial, Singapore 238467

Cambridge University Press is part of Cambridge University Press & Assessment, a department of the University of Cambridge.

We share the University's mission to contribute to society through the pursuit of education, learning and research at the highest international levels of excellence.

www.cambridge.org
Information on this title: www.cambridge.org/9781009619592

DOI: 10.1017/9781009407069

© Çağlayan Başer 2025

This publication is in copyright. Subject to statutory exception and to the provisions of relevant collective licensing agreements, no reproduction of any part may take place without the written permission of Cambridge University Press & Assessment.

When citing this work, please include a reference to the DOI 10.1017/9781009407069

First published 2025

A catalogue record for this publication is available from the British Library

ISBN 978-1-009-61959-2 Hardback
ISBN 978-1-009-40704-5 Paperback
ISSN 2753-8117 (online)
ISSN 2753-8109 (print)

Cambridge University Press & Assessment has no responsibility for the persistence or accuracy of URLs for external or third-party internet websites referred to in this publication and does not guarantee that any content on such websites is, or will remain, accurate or appropriate.

For EU product safety concerns, contact us at Calle de José Abascal, 56, 1°, 28003 Madrid, Spain, or email eugpsr@cambridge.org

Public Preferences, Gender, and Foreign Support for Armed Movements

Elements in Gender and Politics

DOI: 10.1017/9781009407069
First published online: December 2025

Çağlayan Başer
Bilkent University

Author for correspondence: Çağlayan Başer, caglayan.baser@bilkent.edu.tr

Abstract: Female combatants are often central to rebel groups' outreach strategies, yet their impact on foreign support remains unclear. This Element examines how the presence of female fighters shapes international perceptions and support, drawing on original survey experiments in the United States and Tunisia as well as cross-national observational data. The findings demonstrate that foreign audiences are more likely to endorse government sponsorship of rebel groups with female combatants, perceiving them as more gender-equal, democratic, and morally legitimate, and as less likely to harm civilians, even when they are agents of political violence. These favorable perceptions, in turn, increase the likelihood that democratic states will offer material support. In addition to establishing gender composition as a factor influencing external support in armed conflicts, this Element contributes to broader debates on the gender equality–peace nexus, humanitarian aid, rebel legitimacy, and gender stereotypes in nontraditional political spheres.

Keywords: civil wars, external support, gender equality, public opinion, rebel outreach

© Çağlayan Başer 2025

ISBNs: 9781009619592 (HB), 9781009407045 (PB), 9781009407069 (OC)
ISSNs: 2753-8117 (online), 2753-8109 (print)

Contents

1 Introduction   1

2 Theoretical Framework   9

3 Foreign Public Opinion toward Female Fighters: Experimental Analysis   26

4 Foreign Power Support and Gender-Diverse Insurgencies: Observational Analysis   50

5 Conclusion   63

   Appendix   70

   References   92

1 Introduction

In February 2017, the US Central Command tweeted photos of Kurdish female militants fighting against ISIS (the Islamic State of Iraq and Syria) with the caption "Ready for the fight" (US Central Command, 2017a). A few minutes later, they followed with another tweet: "By popular demand, more photos of the female fighters of the Syrian anti-ISIS campaign" (US Central Command, 2017b). Notwithstanding the concerns of Turkey, a NATO (North Atlantic Treaty Organization) ally that considers the Kurdish group a terrorist organization and a vital national security threat, the US did not hesitate to demonstrate open support for them. Similarly, the French President and the Swedish Defense Minister officially welcomed Nesrin Abdullah, the commander of the YPJ, an all-women Kurdish fighting unit of the Democratic Union Party of Syria (PYD). Prioritizing anti-ISIS efforts over allied concerns may seem routine within counterterrorism and geopolitical strategy, but this focus would overlook a crucial gendered aspect: how showcasing female fighters can be strategically used to shape international perceptions, gather public support, and legitimize foreign policy moves by appealing to progressive or moral values.

Alongside official channels, Kurdish female fighters also attracted significant popular international attention. Major Western media outlets, including CNN, BBC, *The Guardian*, PBS, and even teen and fashion magazines like *Teen Vogue* and *Marie-Claire*, featured Kurdish female fighters, celebrating their bravery and highlighting the extraordinary nature of women taking up arms (Griffin, 2014). Headlines read "Women, Life, Freedom" (Lazarus, 2019), "ISIS's Biggest Fear Is Being Killed by Girls" (Webster, 2015), and "A Bullet Almost Killed This Kurdish Sniper. Then She Laughed About It" (Horton, 2017).

Examples of women militants attracting international attention are bountiful (Darden, Henshaw, and Szekely, 2019). Women participate as combatants in over one-third of contemporary armed rebellions, and as noncombatants in two-thirds, impacting conflict dynamics in unique ways (Loken and Matfess, 2024; Wood and Thomas, 2017). Female insurgents receive more sensationalized media coverage than men, which enhances their propaganda value (Sjoberg, 2018) and raises the likelihood of attacks conducted by females, as these actions are expected to gain widespread attention in the Western media (Weeraratne, 2023). Indeed, an essential aspect of rebels' public engagement efforts often involves the intentional inclusion of women insurgents. Many women actively participate in international propaganda activities (Başer, 2022) and use media to raise awareness about their cause (Stallman and Hadi, 2025). From Tigray People's Liberation Front (TPLF) in Ethiopia to Farabundo Martí National Liberation Front (FMLN) in Peru, and Liberation of Tamil Tigers

Eelam (LTTE), numerous rebel organizations promote their female fighters to attract third-party support, sometimes even exaggerating the prevalence of their women militants. For instance, the UN Mission in Nepal reported that Maoists inflated the proportion of women, nearly doubling the actual figure to boost international propaganda (Ortega, 2010: 25). Despite such emphasis on showcasing women by rebel organizations, whether women-focused outreach activities resonate with audiences or translate into tangible support remains unclear.

Rebel groups seek support from foreign patrons to increase their chances of success. Research on external support in civil wars typically focuses on the supply side – the strategic calculus of foreign governments – at the expense of rebels' agency, and tends to ignore why rebels spend considerable resources on outreach activities instead of concentrating on frontline gains (Huang, 2016). Rebels lobby abroad, hire public relations experts, establish international offices, and leverage media platforms to attract support from international actors (Huang, 2016).

For example, the Syrian Democratic Council – the political wing of the Syrian Democratic Forces (SDF) – maintains a mission in Washington, DC, and uses gender equality as a key element of its appeal. Its website states:

> Studies show that peace agreements are more likely to succeed when women participate, and that greater political and social empowerment of women is essential for combating extremism and building free and fair societies. As the only actor in Syria to prioritize women's rights and implement pro-women policies on the ground, we believe our laws and policies are a model for the future of the country that the world should support.[1]

This rhetoric mirrors the gender-progressive stance embraced by international communities, especially among democracies, positioning the SDF not just as a military force but as a promoter of democratic and gender-inclusive values. It highlights how rebels fight not only on the battlefield but also in the arena of international legitimacy, presenting themselves as aligned with liberal democratic ideals. The money and effort spent on these outreach activities suggest that these strategies are integral to how conflicts unravel – yet their impact remains understudied.

This Element fills this gap by evaluating how the gendered imagery of rebel organizations influences foreign perceptions and foreign policy decisions to support them. It focuses on foreign public opinion toward female combatants and its impact on foreign governmental support for civil wars.

Understanding whether and how rebels' gendered outreach strategies affect foreign public opinion and external support matters for several reasons. First, external support is essential for rebel goals such as maintaining territorial

---

[1] Syrian Democratic Council US Mission, www.syriandemocraticcouncil.us/women/.

control, attaining international recognition, inclusion in peace talks, prolonging conflict, and imposing sanctions on adversaries (Caspersen, 2009; Regan, 2002; Stanton, 2016). To attract support, rebels "market" themselves to transnational patrons (Bob, 2005). Understanding how rebels succeed in securing international approval and external support requires examining the factors leading to successful marketing strategies attracting this support.

Second, policymakers, especially in democracies, are responsive to domestic preferences, including foreign policy decisions and the use of force, making them wary of foreign adventurism (Baum and Potter, 2015; Chu and Recchia, 2022). Supporting a violent group responsible for civilian casualties can serve as fodder for the domestic opposition to undermine government approval and damage the international reputation of a democratic state. Public perceptions are critical here because foreign armed groups lack the legitimacy of an allied state (Kreps and Maxey, 2018). Yet, public reaction toward external support for nonstate armed groups has attracted limited attention.

Third, although there is limited empirical evidence on how women involved in conflict are viewed, the political psychology literature widely recognizes that gender stereotypes shape assessments of female politicians. Traditional norms often depict female politicians as ethical, nurturing, and passive (Kahn 1996), whereas male politicians as assertive leaders are better suited for "hard" issues like security or economy (Dolan, 2010). While some recent work demonstrates the persistence of these stereotypes (Aaldering and Van der Pas, 2020; O'Brien, 2019), disadvantaging women in elections across Western and non-Western contexts (Blackman and Jackson 2021; Liu, 2018), others find no negative bias toward females in the political sphere (Adams et al., 2023; Schwarz and Coppock, 2022), even suggesting that women can be viewed as more capable than men even in traditionally male domains (Lust and Benstead, 2024). This mixed evidence on gender bias in political participation raises questions about whether similar stereotypes might shape attitudes toward female actors in conflict contexts, where perceptions of capability and suitability for "hard" issues like security could be particularly significant. How such gendered understandings impact attitudes in conflict contexts remains understudied.

War is often seen as the continuation of politics by other means (von Clausewitz, [1832] 1873); however, patriarchal mechanisms dominate war settings much more than they do traditional politics. Men are viewed as natural warriors, whereas women are associated with peace, nonviolence, and passivity. Further, "ambiguity is endemic to civil wars," and uncertainty about actors' intentions, aims, and methods is more prevalent in conflict settings than in traditional politics (Kalyvas 2003: 476). The literature on gender stereotypes in traditional politics suggests that people should rely on these stereotypes to make judgments about conflict. Yet, we know little about which stereotypes inform citizens' attitudes in conflict settings, to what extent, and how. Understanding how people evaluate gender in rebel groups would contribute to the political psychology scholarship by informing us about how people make judgments in low-information and hypermasculine political settings.

Fourth, assessing which gendered beliefs are reproduced in conflict settings is crucial because these beliefs can contribute to the legitimacy of the organizations (Viterna, 2014). Gender-diverse cadres can appeal to foreign audiences and be leveraged by the rebels as the embodiment of gender-equal policies to humanize the groups. Building legitimacy is critical for the international approval of rebel groups because rebels who appear legitimate can better attract external support and, thus, favorable conflict outcomes (Jo, 2015; Stanton, 2020).

This Element fills these theoretical and empirical gaps by dissecting the relationship between gender roles, public opinion, and foreign conflict assistance. Particularly, I answer the following questions: How does women's visible presence in insurgent groups affect foreign support? Do the rebel groups with women fighters attract more support than those without? If so, through which mechanisms does support operate?

I argue that the presence of women sends signals about the rebel group's characteristics that are different from those of male rebels because traditional gender stereotypes associate men and women with different traits. The gender of rebel group members functions as a heuristic, informing people about the characteristics of the conflict environment, especially in the absence of further information, where there is uncertainty about rebel characteristics. Through survey experiments in different sociopolitical contexts, I examine whether foreign publics prefer supporting groups with female combatants and assess the mechanisms of this preference. Then, using observational cross-national data, I examine whether foreign public attitudes toward female combatants can translate into actual external government support for gender-diverse armed groups.

Traditional gender stereotypes are especially influential in conflict, with citizens often favoring "strong," masculine leaders in times of war or security threats (Barnes and O'Brien, 2018; Lawless, 2004), while women are deemed to be nurturing peacemakers or passive victims (Sjoberg and Gentry, 2007). These stereotypes can fuel competing perceptions of rebel groups with female fighters: foreign audiences may dismiss them as weaker and less capable of military success or, conversely, view them as more moderate and morally righteous. Drawing on literatures on social psychology, foreign policy, conflict, gender politics, public opinion, and media studies, I explore how the presence of female militants in rebel groups shapes foreign public perceptions, and garners favorable perceptions even when those groups employ violent strategies that audiences typically disapprove of. The presence of female combatants acts as a gendered signal, shaping perceptions by evoking entrenched expectations of women as peaceful or morally virtuous. Women's agency in violence creates a cognitive inconsistency that observers resolve by projecting traits like moderation onto the entire group. Media and rebel outreach amplify these entrenched associations, presenting women as mothers, victims, or brave women's rights activists. This enhances the group's appeal to foreign audiences and increases foreign support for their rebel groups.

To analyze how conveying the message about the presence of women insurgents attracts support from third parties, first, I conduct original survey experiments in the US and Tunisia to assess micro-foundations of foreign attitudes toward sponsoring gender-diverse armed groups and parse out the mechanisms through which foreign audiences evaluate women's presence in insurgencies differently from that of male rebels. I examine attitudes toward various forms of foreign support – verbal endorsement, economic aid, military intervention, and refugee acceptance – to pinpoint the extent of female combatants' impact and to assess whether certain types of assistance are more affected by the gender composition of rebel groups.

The results from these two different geographic and cultural contexts provide direct evidence that foreign audiences are more likely to support their government's sponsorship of these groups when they know about female combatants' presence. I find that this effect is particularly pronounced in the US, where citizens express stronger support for governmental endorsement – in terms of both verbal and financial backing – and are more open to accepting refugees from conflict zones when women participate in combat. The findings also reveal that both American and Tunisian respondents strongly perceive rebel groups recruiting women as more gender-equal and democratic. Additionally, they are more likely to view these groups as using less violence against civilians and see their armed struggle as more morally justifiable. These normative and humanitarian perceptions are central mechanisms driving public support for gender-diverse organizations. Contrary to expectations of backlash against women stepping into combat roles, there is no evidence of such a reaction. On the contrary, those with more traditional gender views – particularly among Tunisians – express stronger support for female combatants, challenging the assumption that conservatism uniformly resists women's participation in conflict

In the second part of the analysis, I examine whether these favorable attitudes influence actual foreign assistance from democracies. I focus on support from democratic states because leaders in these countries are more responsive to public opinion. As observed in the experiment, the presence of female fighters signals democracy and gender equality, making it easier for democratic leaders to justify support for these groups as consistent with national principles. Based on observational evidence from a global sample of rebel organizations between 1989 and 2009, I show that groups with female combatants are more likely to receive support from democratic states. Overall, evidence from two sets of analyses suggests that female participation in armed groups can attract tangible international benefits for rebel groups; sponsoring organizations with female fighters would be less likely to be considered an act of adventurism by foreign audiences, and the presence of female fighters can give the leaders an option of attaching a moral spin to the decision to support the rebel group.

The findings advance several key areas of research. First, this Element contributes both theoretically and empirically to the burgeoning literature on the outcomes of women's participation in conflict (Başer, 2022; Braithwaite and Ruiz, 2018; Brannon, 2023; Giri and Haer, 2024; Loken, 2024; Manekin and Wood, 2020; Wood and Allemang, 2022). Theoretically, it identifies specific mechanisms through which gendered outreach by rebel groups prompts external support, yielding tangible benefits. Empirically, it quantifies these benefits' impact on foreign support through survey experiments with diverse audiences holding varying perspectives on women's public roles. This way, it establishes the micro-foundations of how female combatants influence external support, positioning it as one of the first to examine female combatants' role in shaping foreign government sponsorship of rebel groups.

A notable exception is Manekin and Wood (2020), who show that female combatants can boost rebel legitimacy, particularly among US citizens, and help attract support from international nongovernmental organizations (INGOs) and diasporas. Building on their work, this Element shifts the focus from legitimacy to exploring how female fighters shape both external public and governmental support through various causal mechanisms: instrumental factors, like sponsor states' reputations and security interests; humanitarian concerns, like civilian harm and repression; and ideological cues, such as democratic or gender-equal imagery. Following their call to examine these dynamics across contexts, I analyze how gender norms and conflict exposure in both Western and Middle Eastern settings shape perceptions of gender-diverse groups, and show that these groups are more likely to gain support from democratic states. Overall, this Element goes beyond existing literature by dissecting how and why women insurgents affect foreign public opinion on different forms of conflict assistance and government support across contexts.

Second, I advance the scholarship on third-party involvement in civil wars by positioning rebel group membership, particularly gender composition, as a determinant of foreign support and parsing out the mechanisms linking them, highlighting the effect of membership in shaping rebel groups' perceived characteristics. Recent experimental research suggests that the traits and behaviors of armed groups influence international audience perceptions, yet few studies have directly investigated how these attitudes are formed (Arves, Cunningham, and McCulloch, 2019) and how these attitudes can translate into actual state support. This Element contributes to the literature on foreign policy attitudes by demonstrating that female combatants can increase foreign support for rebel groups by signaling humanitarian values and ideological moderation, aligning with research on the role of moral considerations in shaping public opinion on intervention (Kertzer et al., 2014; Kreps and Maxey, 2018). It also adds to scholarship on the international appeal of rebel groups by showing how gendered signals, such as the inclusion of women, enhance perceptions of a group's humanitarian profile, a factor crucial for securing international legitimacy and support (Jo, 2015; Jo, Yi, and Barrett, 2025; Stanton, 2016).

Third, by exploring female combatants' role in public opinion, this Element furthers our understanding on the consequences of women's participation beyond formal politics. Research on women's political representation suggests that women politicians evoke positive perceptions regarding legitimate and honest governance (Barnes and Beaulieu, 2019; Clayton, O'Brien, and Piscopo, 2019; Kao et al., 2024). This Element shows that women's participation incites similar positive perceptions in nontraditional realms of politics, even when they are perpetrators of violence and in traditionally masculine settings. Although rebel groups typically lack free and fair elections and tend not to prioritize gender rights, women's participation makes their armed rebellion appear more democratic and gender equal. This Element suggests that these gendered views are so embedded that they are echoed in conflict settings and alter the conflict dynamics. Contrary to expectations of societal pushback against women breaking traditional norms by participating in combat, the results indicate that the presence of female combatants enhances group support, sometimes even more among those with conservative views. Hence, it extends research on gender stereotypes by showing that perceptions of good governance pertaining to female leaders in formal politics also apply to insurgencies, and that these gendered perceptions travel across formal politics and conflict settings.

Fourth, this Element advances and problematizes the broader empirical studies showing a positive association between women, gender equality, and peace. Studies show that states with higher gender equality are less likely to engage in conflict – referred to as the "gender equality–peace hypothesis" (Caprioli and Boyer, 2001; Hudson et al., 2009; Melander, 2005; Wood and Ramirez, 2018). Studies also show that women are typically less supportive of the use of force in foreign policy compared to men, even when controlling for factors like political partisanship, income, education, and age – referred to as the gender gap in support of war or as the "women–peace hypothesis" (Eichenberg, 2016; McDermott and Cowden, 2001; Tessler and Warriner, 1997). However, these attitudes are almost always assessed when perpetrators are male or presumed to be male – as the default image of a soldier or rebel is typically male. This Element complicates these hypotheses by revealing that violent organizations with female combatants are often perceived as embracing gender equality, leading people to support, and even endorse, military intervention on behalf of these groups, despite their violent tactics. In other words, gender equality can sustain support for armed groups and their violent tactics. This is puzzling because feminist consciousness – often considered central to women's opposition to war (Brooks and Valentino, 2011) – appears here to increase support for gender-diverse violent groups, challenging the assumption that gender equality and aversion to conflict go hand in hand.

Fifth, this Element contributes to the literature on gendered political preferences by showing that the gender gap in support of political violence disappears when combatants are women, which challenges the women–peace hypothesis. In other words, women are more prone to support using force when they see that their same-gender counterparts are engaged in combat. Despite female respondents' lower baseline support levels for insurgencies, both male and female respondents show greater support when female fighters are involved, suggesting that gender representation in combat can shift women's perspectives on conflict. The results suggest that the differences in individual gendered attitudes toward violence should not be evaluated independently from the gender of the perpetrator. These results highlight a complex relationship between gender and conflict, where the presence of female fighters and support for gender equality can foster, rather than diminish, support for violence. Overall, this examination of the relationship between gender roles, public opinion, and conflict responds to scholars' calls to focus on mechanisms to have more refined theories about gender and political violence (Cohen and Karim, 2022).

In the rest of the Element, I first theorize about how the presence of female insurgents leads to a significantly different perspective on a rebel organization. Particularly, in Section 2, I explore how information on the gender of militants is processed to reveal positive or negative perceptions about the entire armed group. Then, I parse out the potential mechanisms through which traits associated with women can impact support for insurgency. In Section 3, I outline the original survey experiment design and present results from both the US and the Tunisian samples, demonstrating that the gender composition of rebel groups primarily influences foreign support by shaping perceptions of the group's humane conduct, ideologies, and values. Section 4 describes the cross-national analysis and discusses the observational evidence, providing proof that groups with female fighters can attract more support from democracies. Finally, in Section 5, I discuss the primary contributions and their implications for research and policymaking.

2 Theoretical Framework

This section establishes the theoretical framework by addressing two questions: (1) Why would female militants' presence affect public support? (2) How, or through which mechanisms, does female militants' presence shape foreign audiences' opinions? First, I outline the underlying premises of the theoretical framework, drawing from social psychology, foreign policy, and media studies literatures to explain why women's presence should make a difference in public opinion. This framework helps us to understand how militants' gender can become an important piece of information in making sense of the conflict dynamics, and why women's visible presence can garner favorable perceptions even when they are just as willing as other groups to employ violent strategies that are frowned upon by foreign audiences. Second, I explore the mechanisms by which female militants affect foreign opinion, drawing on the scholarship from foreign conflict assistance and gender politics. In doing so, I discuss examples from media coverage and rebel activities to illustrate how these narratives converge to shape external perceptions of female militants.

2.1 Why Would Female Militants' Presence Affect Public Support? Processing Information on Militants' Gender

Militants' gender can sway public opinion and impact decisions on sponsoring rebel groups. Foreign policy scholarship maintains that the information available to foreign leaders and the public is often disproportionate, with the latter having less access (Baum and Potter, 2008). When making political judgments, people rely on the heuristic cues available to them to compensate for limited information (Popkin, 1994). Especially in conflict situations where uncertainty – about the goals, characteristics, strategies, and actions of actors – is pervasive, people use heuristics to infer the goals and natures of the warring parties.

The gender of militants is an important cue for audiences, to help them form beliefs about the conflict about which they lack context. All social identities – such as racial, ethnic, and gender – are associated with a set of norms that prescribe the expected behavior for members of that category. These norms and expectations influence behavior because they affect individuals' preferences. The perceived social identity of rebel members thereby works as a shortcut, informing people about the characteristics of the conflict environment, such as how they behave, what they are fighting for, and what they are up against.

That said, women constitute a smaller fraction of combatants in contemporary rebellions. While their noncombatant roles are more common, they participate as fighters in about one-third of armed movements, with 15 percent of rebel groups having a dedicated women's wing with frontline units exclusively for female fighters (Matfess and Loken, 2024; Wood and Thomas, 2017). Despite their relatively limited presence, how can female combatants convey so much about the entire group's character, shaping opinions on backing the group?

Social psychology literature suggests that individual traits can serve as powerful cognitive shortcuts for identifying the whole group to which those individuals belong, a phenomenon known as "entitativity" (Campbell, 1958). Entitativity refers to the perception of a collection of people as bonded together in a meaningful unit (Crawford, Sherman, and Hamilton, 2002). This perception of group unity prompts observers to use the available information to infer dispositional qualities in the target group, form a cohesive impression of the group, assume consistency across situations, and attempt to resolve any inconsistencies in the information about the group (Hamilton and Sherman, 1996). For instance, spectators at a soccer game, though not an organized group, are often seen as having high entitativity; people attribute traits like aggressiveness to all fans based on the actions of a few, viewing them as a unified – and aggressive – group (Campbell, 1958). Entitativity is a crucial precursor to stereotyping, especially for outgroups with so-called essential identities that are perceived as fixed, like gender or race. This is particularly the case when only a few individuals are visible in a field (e.g., women in the military), where they stand out as "tokens" (Agadullina and Lovakov 2018; Crawford et al., 2002).

In conflict settings, the entitativity mechanism leads to stereotyping that extends characteristics associated with women to the entire rebel organization. The involvement of women as perpetrators of violence disrupts the conventional view of women as inherently peaceful. This creates cognitive inconsistency. Observers may resolve this inconsistency by projecting stereotypical female traits onto the entire rebel group, simplifying complex conflict dynamics into familiar gendered beliefs.

This stereotype projection can take two forms: Observers may attribute traditionally "feminine" traits, such as compassion or nurturance, to the group, assuming that women's presence makes the group more peaceful. Alternatively, women's violent roles may clash with gender norms, leading to perceptions of female combatants as deviants and their groups as morally corrupt. How the group is ultimately perceived – favorably or unfavorably – depends on (i) the pervasiveness of gender roles, (ii) the media framing, and (iii) the rebels' international outreach activities.[2] The pervasiveness of embedded gender norms suggests that people are likely to assign their preexisting gendered assumptions to the rebel group upon seeing women as part of it, even absent information – that is, with a lack of media framing or strategic rebel propaganda. That said, media framing and rebels' intentional gendered strategies solidify these perceptions. I will now unpack each of these factors.

First, the pervasiveness of gender roles is one way that the process of stereotype projection to an entire group operates. The link between women, peace, and morality is so deeply ingrained that it underpins national identity and shapes notions of citizenship (Peterson, 1992). Scholars posit that concepts of state and citizenship cannot be understood without considering gender; women are envisaged as moral authorities, entrusted with guarding and passing national identity to generations (Yuval-Davis, 1997). People readily rely on these embedded norms even more in contexts with ambiguity about actors' responsibilities. Ambiguity encourages cognitive distortion aligned with traditional gender norms (Heilman and Haynes, 2005), reinforcing perceptions that women are more peaceful and moral than men. This reinforces the "peaceful woman" stereotype, even when women engage in violence, and shapes beliefs about the rebel group's behavior (as more peaceful), helping people solve the inconsistency in seeing women as part of a violent group.

Second, media framing amplifies these perceptions by leveraging gendered frames. The mainstream media, along with elites, plays a crucial role in shaping public attitudes toward foreign policy (Entman, 2003). The media reports news through specific frames that cue the receiver to contextualize events, using selective issues, words, and photographs to influence how the story is perceived. Despite the diversity of contemporary media outlets, framing usually aligns with entrenched audience predispositions, as the media seeks to satisfy public demand as a strategic actor (Baum and Potter, 2008). Framing a news item is most potent when it is culturally congruent with schemes that most members of society habitually employ (Entman, 2003), and emotionally charged news influences foreign policy attitudes more than sole information (Gadarian, 2010).

---

[2] Though the group's ideology and its affinity with one's country, when such knowledge is available, would also be important factors shaping perceptions.

While the demand for foreign policy–related news is typically low, especially in the US, several factors capture public interest, such as casualty levels and elite discord (Baum and Potter, 2008). The presence of female fighters is one such case that prompts public attention. They garner more sensational and emotional media coverage than men, which increases their propaganda value for rebels (Nacos, 2005). For instance, in recent conflicts in Syria and Iraq, women have been "hypervisible," becoming central figures in media coverage (Sjoberg, 2018).

Despite pursuing different objectives, mainstream media reporting and rebel outreach strategies often rely on similar frameworks to engage the public; both reinforce and are shaped by existing gendered expectations. In conflict, when women participate as combatants, the Western media in particular portrays them as mothers, victims, or feminists in romanticized narratives that evoke emotions aligned with socially resonant gendered themes (Sjoberg and Gentry, 2007; Toivanen and Baser, 2016). This framing corroborates the gendered framing by rebel groups, emphasizing women's bravery, motherhood, and peacefulness (Rajan, 2011). This depiction reinforces the "peaceful women" stereotype even when women engage in violence; it downplays the severity of their violent acts, portraying them as victims of harsh conditions (more so than males) or as advocates for gender equality (detailed in Section 3).[3]

Third, rebel groups are usually aware of the propaganda value of female militants, and strategically deploy them for international support. Typically, groups recruit women not just for international outreach but for other advantages as well, including expanding the labor force, building ties with locals, and, as they can more easily bypass security checks, aiding covert operations such as espionage, recruitment, and weapons transport. However, groups are also aware of women's outreach advantages and make strategic choices to attract external support.

For example, the LTTE leadership was keenly aware of the impact that armed women could have on foreign perceptions of the movement's objectives and actively promoted them through various media (Wood, 2019). Its international branches produced and distributed documentaries, published books and

---

[3] Both media and rebel groups can manipulate entitativity, increasing the effectiveness of the message. The media can shape perceptions of groups' unity by emphasizing coordinated efforts, shared objectives, or strong leadership. The media's "episodic framing" – focusing on individuals and stories lacking context – reduces perceived entitativity, while "thematic framing" – rich in context, highlighting collective structures – enhances it (Iyengar, 1991). Rebel organizations typically aspire to look more coherent, like political parties, rather than like sprawling clandestine networks, and so often maintain just a few centrally controlled websites.

magazines highlighting women's roles, and arranged media interviews with female militants (Brun, 2005). United Nations reports revealed that Nepal's Maoists inflated female militants' numbers to almost double for international propaganda purposes (Ortega, 2010). Gerakan Aceh Merdeka (GAM) in Indonesia coordinated with Western media to promote its limited number of female combatants to foreigners (Manekin and Wood, 2020). The leader of the Kurdistan Workers' Party (PKK – Partiya Karkerên Kurdistanê, in Kurdish), Öcalan, also recognized the role of women in mobilizing international support. From its early years, the PKK cultivated ties with global women's organizations, securing the women's military unit's (YAJK) participation in the 1995 UN World Conference on Women (Başer, 2022). Öcalan frequently credited women with shaping global perceptions, emphasizing in the PKK's official bulletin that they elevated the group's appeal and image in Europe and the Middle East (PKK, 2001: 7). He specifically highlights the Kurdish women's resistance against ISIS as a turning point, stating that their courage significantly amplified international attention for PKK (Başer, 2022).

These examples illustrate how the media, rebel strategies, and public attitudes interact. Rebels leverage gendered outreach to attract support, while audiences, influenced by ingrained gender biases, interpret female militants in ways that align with preexisting perceptions. Since media portrayals and rebel messaging are rarely neutral, their interaction likely amplifies the effect of female combatants far more than controlled experimental settings can capture.

However, not all women would give the same impression. A group's ideology and whether it shares an affinity with one's country, when such information is available, are important factors shaping perceptions. I expect the theorized relationship to be weak or absent in cases such as women in veils, women depicted as suicide bombers, and abducted women. The veil symbolizes Islam, and female militants linked to groups espousing extremist interpretations of Islam are usually vilified or viewed as mentally ill, as depicted in racialized portrayals in the Western media. Female suicide bombers killing civilians tend to be evaluated negatively compared to women, for instance, engaging in guerrilla warfare. They are often portrayed as mad, or monsters, drastically deviating from feminine nurturing norms (Gentry and Sjoberg, 2015). These portrayals vilify rather than humanize them, dampening their appeal to audiences. Also, the dynamics discussed here apply more to women who join armed groups voluntarily, as abducted women are less likely to gain support by signaling peace, nonviolence, or gender progressiveness. Uganda's Lord's Resistance Army (LRA) gained notoriety for abducting thousands, forcing them into child soldiering or sexual slavery, which undermined support. Yet, without such information, people would likely assume voluntary participation.[4]

Women in noncombatant roles are less likely to attract international attention or support because women serving as cooks, cleaners, nurses, or messengers, while essential to the functioning of the group, do not challenge traditional gender norms in the same way as combatants. They are less likely to be framed as markers of progressivism, empowerment, or humanitarian concern than the combatant women who visibly break norms. Noncombatant women are also less likely to raise negative perceptions about military capability, as they do not engage in fighting. Hence, they may evoke weaker emotional or ideological reactions – whether about equality or concern about military power. Overall, while their roles are crucial, they remain largely out of the international spotlight and are less likely to change public opinion. While these are plausible, further research is needed to explore the impact of these various forms of women's participation in conflict on international audiences. For instance, some noncombat roles, such as nurses, can still trigger humanitarian emotions, especially if they are framed well by advocacy campaigns and rebel lobbyists. This Element, however, focuses on women in combatant, rather than noncombatant, roles, where their involvement in violence sharply contradicts traditional gender norms.

Another question is to whom the rebels are signaling and whether their strategies vary by audience. Rebels can leverage different reputation-building strategies to appeal to different constituencies (Akcinaroglu and Tokdemir, 2018). For instance, service provision strengthens legitimacy among locals, while compliance with international law boosts international standing. However, they can seek legitimacy from both, making the efforts interconnected. Rebels seeking local authority also engage with humanitarian actors, as international backing weakens state narratives (Jo et al., 2025). In this context, the gender norms of their audience would shape how rebels market female combatants, as they would tailor narratives to align with their targets' values. For example, the PKK emphasized its gender-progressivism in engaging with Western democracies, while embodying traditional norms in its local communications, portraying women as primarily mothers and symbols of innocence to raise sympathy and reinforce ceasefire credibility (Başer, 2022). Szekely (2020) contends that, in the Syrian Civil War, rebel groups and states deployed female combatants as a cost-effective means of signaling alignment with the US and differentiating themselves from ISIS. They also manipulated the visibility of

---

[4] However, if conflict is characterized by high levels of abduction, like Boko Haram, audiences (especially informed or domestic) may assume that women have been forcefully recruited.

women, emphasizing or minimizing their presence to appeal to different audiences. As such, we would expect rebels seeking support from liberal democracies to be more likely to convey egalitarian messaging than those courting actors like Saudi Arabia, where such narratives hold less appeal.

Another question is whether there's a gap between rebels' marketing strategies and the experiences of female militants. Organizations can embrace gender equality as both a normative commitment and a strategic tool (Başer, 2022). Even without genuine commitment, the presence of women fighters can project an egalitarian image, but this risks backlash if seen as inauthentic. Scholars disagree on whether armed groups can truly cultivate gender emancipation. Sixta (2008) views female militants as First Wave feminists, arguing that they resist triple oppression – Western, societal, and organizational. Others maintain that even groups promoting gender equality often remain patriarchal, abandon reforms post-conflict, and expose women to new vulnerabilities (Mazurana et al., 2002). Recent research shows mixed outcomes: group-level studies find that women can advocate for designing and implementing inclusive peace deals (Brannon and Thomas, forthcoming; Thomas, 2024), while individual-level accounts, like in FARC (Revolutionary Armed Forces of Colombia), highlight how women's newfound greater agency remains constrained by collective goals and patriarchal (Barrios Sabogal, 2021). This agency is also shaped by intersectional factors like class, ethnicity, and education, as in the Nepal Maoists (Giri, 2023). This Element doesn't aim to judge whether rebels' gendered messaging is genuine or if female fighters are actually empowered, but it argues that associations between women and values like equality, peace, and moderation, amplified by media and rebel narratives, can shape support for their groups.

Overall, insights from social psychology, public opinion on foreign policy, and the media indicate that information about militants' gender should systematically influence public opinion. It follows that the gender of rebel membership matters for conflict dynamics, as the presence of women makes a difference in how rebel groups are perceived. In the next section, I outline pathways through which women and their rebel groups can shape perceptions and influence foreign support, walking through examples from media framing and rebel outreach strategies.

2.2 How Does Female Militants' Presence Shape Foreign Audiences' Opinions? Mechanisms of Support for Female Combatants

After establishing *why* messages of women combatants would shape public perceptions differently than male insurgents, this section explains *how*, or through which mechanisms, they affect foreign audience's opinions. Public support for foreign conflict assistance is influenced by both normative and instrumental concerns (Holsti, 2004). Normatively, individuals are more likely to support interventions framed around humanitarian values – such as protecting civilians or aiding groups perceived as morally just or those linked to their ideologies and core values (Kertzer and Zeitzoff, 2017; Kreps and Maxey, 2018). On the other hand, instrumental support is often contingent on expected national benefits or gains on the ground (Gelpi, Feaver, and Reifler, 2009).

The traits associated with women can potentially impact foreign public support for the insurgency through both normative and instrumental concerns, which can pull the support in either direction. Normatively, groups with female combatants increase public support as they are considered to exercise moderation, pursue just goals, and/or support gender equality. Yet, instrumental concerns can either increase or decrease support. Specifically, citizens' concerns about their country's international reputation can increase support, while doubts about practical gains may decrease it, as women are often viewed as unfit for combat.

Building on scholarship on foreign conflict assistance and gendered conflict dynamics, I outline mechanisms through which female combatants can shape public support for foreign armed movements in three groups: (1) humanitarian concerns, (2) ideologies and values, and (3) instrumental concerns. I divide the normative concerns into the first two categories, as doing so clarifies distinct pathways through which gendered assumptions can shape support – namely through ethical obligations surrounding conflict dynamics versus alignment with the group's values. Table 1 outlines the underlying factors driving foreign public support for conflict assistance, the gendered assumptions amplifying these factors, and the expected support trends for groups with female combatants based on these drivers. To the best of my knowledge, no studies have systematically tested these perceptions about female fighters or how these perceptions increase or decrease public support for their government's backing of the group.

2.2.1 Humanitarian Concerns

Humanitarian and moral imperatives influence citizens' support for war (Tomz and Weeks, 2020). Among these concerns, civilian casualty, moral war conduct, and proportionality among warring parties stand out as they reflect key war norms, and women's involvement makes these concerns even more pronounced. Due to women's image as nonviolent, civilian, victim, and moral figures, their presence can increase support for their armed rebellions.

Table 1 Mechanisms of support driven by the gender of the insurgents

Foundations	Public support drivers	Gendered assumptions	Expectations
Humanitarian concerns	**Civilian casualties:** People care about civilian suffering.	Women are associated with nonviolence and civilians.	Support increases as people think that the group uses *less civilian violence*.
	Moral conduct: People prefer morally just conduct in war strategies.	Women are seen as more moral.	Support increases as people think that the group is *more morally justified*.
	Repression: People prefer proportionality among warring parties.	Severe repression leads women to fight.	Support increases as people think that the group faces *higher repression*.
Ideologies and values	**Democracy:** People value democracy.	Women's presence suggests democratic principles.	Support increases as people think that the group embraces *democratic principles*.
	Gender equality: People value women's rights.	Women's presence indicates respect for women's rights.	Support increases as people think that the group embraces *gender equality*.
Instrumental concerns	**Strategic viability:** People support likely successful rebels that advance their country's strategic interests.	Women's presence suggests military weakness.	Support decreases as people think that the insurgency lacks *military capacity* and that sponsoring the insurgency hurts the *security interests* of their country.
	Reputation: People care about their country's global reputation.	Supporting female combatants boosts the sponsor's reputation.	Support increases as people think that sponsoring the group boosts their country's *reputation*.

The first mechanism under the humanitarian-concern category is about harm inflicted upon civilians in combat zones. Protection of civilians is an international norm; Geneva Conventions require fighting parties to strictly refrain from targeting civilians. Research shows that civilian casualties reduce support for use of force (Gartner, 2008; Kertzer et al., 2014).

People may associate women with civilians and nonviolence, which can boost support for female combatants. Prevalent gender norms deem men to be the natural warriors while attributing victim or civilian roles to women. The phrase "women and children" best exemplifies how women are framed as civilians, innocent, and in need of protection, akin to children. Strategically employed by INGOs to attract donors (Carpenter, 2005), the phrase suggests that women lack agency and share children's vulnerability to violence, rather than being potential fighters. These presumptions can lead people to evaluate groups recruiting women as *less likely to attack civilians*, which can increase support for their groups.

The second mechanism through which women can impact war support is proportionality of the use of force among warring parties, or state repression in civil wars (Hurka, 2005). Walzer's (1977) classic work on war ethics highlights the proportionality principle, where warring parties should refrain from using excessive or disproportionate force vis-à-vis their military objective. Research suggests that citizens also care about proportionality in conflict, shaping their support for the use of force (Dill, Sagan, and Valentino, 2022).

Public sensitivity to proportionality suggests that perceptions of force's scale matter. Traditional norms associate women with motherhood, passivity, and innocence, rather than being active political agents, so their involvement in combat signals extraordinary circumstances. When women take up arms, it indicates that repression is so severe that even the most passive members of society are compelled to fight. Scholars presume that this perception of disproportionate force against women helps groups with female combatants build legitimacy and mobilize support (Loken, 2021; Viterna, 2014). This, in turn, can raise public sympathy for the group, as observers may view women's participation as evidence of disproportionate state violence, increasing favorability toward the group.

The third mechanism is shaping perceptions of the group's cause as morally justified. Research shows that public support for US foreign policy decisions rises when framed around supporting human rights, and beliefs about the moral righteousness of conflict intervention drive support for foreign assistance more than strategic concerns (Kreps and Maxey, 2018).

Women are typically considered the "fairer sex," which can shape people's understanding of conflict dynamics, as it does in politics. People tend to view female politicians as less corrupt and more honest than their male counterparts, with their involvement enhancing the legitimacy of political decisions (Barnes and Beaulieu, 2019; Clayton et al., 2019). Similarly, female-led parties are perceived as more moderate than male-led parties (O'Brien, 2019). These assumptions extend to conflict settings, where women are believed to have a similar moderating effect on rebel group perceptions (MacKenzie, 2009). Perceptions linking women with moral behaviors can lead people to view groups with female combatants as fighting a more *moral cause* than their male-dominated counterparts, bolstering support for the group.

Media Coverage and Rebel Outreach: How can women maintain their nonviolent, victim, and ethical image even when they are perpetrators of violence? Media portrayals, often aligned with rebel outreach strategies, play a key role. Especially the Western mainstream media's framing of women militants reinforces the existing perceptions associating women with morally desirable notions. For example, a *New York Times* article on the uprising against Qaddafi emphasizes the legitimacy and inclusivity that the women bring to the armed rebellion: "Perhaps most important, women here participated in such large numbers they helped establish the legitimacy of the revolution, demonstrating that support for the uprising has penetrated deep into Libyan society" (Barnard, 2011). Another news title in the *Independent* emphasizes the motherhood of rebels: "Female Yemeni fighters carry babies and machine guns at the anti-Saudi rally" (Pasha-Robinson, 2017). Sputnik's choice to include an interview of a male insurgent fighting in the Syrian Civil War illustrates how motherhood traits are attached to female fighters, even though the organization effectively bans motherhood by prohibiting sexual relationships: "There are true heroes among women. They display courage on the battlefield while giving birth. That is what infuses a woman with greatness. Allah gave them qualities men do not have" (Sputnik International, 2015).

Toivanen and Baser (2016) find that the French and the British media portray Kurdish female fighters as selfless defenders, using violence only as a last resort, thus underscoring the severity of repression. The Western media often frames non-Western women as needing liberation (Macdonald, 2006), while novels depict female terrorists sympathetically, balancing their roles as both life-givers and life-takers through maternal compassion (McManus, 2013). These portrayals suggest that the Western media tends to present female rebels favorably, appealing to emotions and reinforcing existing beliefs, thus enhancing their propaganda value.

Rebel groups align with these portrayals to evoke humanitarian concerns, often leveraging motherhood to soften perceptions of violence (Viterna, 2014). They use imagery of mothers holding rifles alongside babies to humanize and justify their cause, emphasizing women's perceived nonviolence (Loken, 2021). For example, a Palestine Liberation Organization (PLO) poster depicts an armed woman as "woman, mother, and fighter on the path to liberation," prioritizing motherhood as her revolutionary identity. This rhetoric spans the political spectrum, with leftist groups like Nicaragua's Sandinistas and South Africa's African National Congress (ANC) employing it despite not advocating traditional gender roles. Similarly, religious fundamentalist groups like Hamas and Hezbollah stress motherhood, despite rarely deploying women in combat (Loken, 2021).

Rebel groups also frame their women fighters as righteous defenders and protectors of vulnerable women. The LTTE highlighted its role in shielding women from sexual violence by Sri Lankan forces (Stack-O'Connor, 2007). In 2013, FARC launched Mujer Fariana to depict its women as empowered fighters defending the oppressed, while al-Qaeda produced a magazine called Al Shamikha ("Majestic Woman") to humanize their cause and downplay violent tactics.

To sum, just as stereotypes in traditional politics shape perceptions of female leaders – viewed as emotional, caring, passive, and gentle versus men as aggressive and forceful – similar perceptions (reinforced by media portrayal and rebel outreach activities) can lead to underestimating civilian targeting, overestimating state repression, and perceiving a more moral cause when female combatants are involved. These favorable perceptions can increase support for gender-diverse armed groups.

2.2.2 Ideologies and Values

Ideologies and values constitute another group of factors that influence public views on foreign policy; people are more likely to support conflict involvement abroad if foreign actors align with their beliefs (Chu, 2021). Among these values, democratic principles and gender equality particularly resonate with citizens in democracies and autocracies – though perhaps to a lesser extent. I argue that the presence of women in rebel groups signals these values, suggesting a commitment to democratic principles and respect for women's rights, which can bolster public support for their government's sponsorship of these groups.

First, democratic principles have become an essential source of these shared ideologies and values among citizens, shaping their attitudes toward support for the use of force abroad. People in democracies are more supportive of intervening on behalf of democracies than of autocracies, and more averse to attacking democracies – this sets the foundation of the democratic peace theory (Tomz and Weeks, 2013). At the same time, women's rights have been associated with democracies. Women's inclusion in political decision-making is seen as essential to democratic governance; it ensures that half the population is represented in decision-making, and enhances perceptions of the fairness, inclusivity, and responsiveness of democratic institutions (Barnes and Beaulieu, 2014; Clayton et al., 2019). These values are reflected among the international community too. As gender equality rose on the global agenda, democracy promotion and foreign aid efforts began to emphasize women's representation. Women's political participation and democratic norms have become so closely bundled that even authoritarian regimes adopt gender quotas to enhance their democratic reputation in the international arena. Research shows that foreign audiences are indeed receptive to this image; they consider countries with higher women's representation to be more democratic, even when countries lack elections (Bush, Donno, and Zetterberg 2024).

This association between women's inclusion and democratic values can extend beyond formal politics into armed conflict. Just as women's representation has become shorthand for democracy in states, the presence of women in rebel groups may signal a similar commitment to democratic norms – whether genuine or strategic. International observers, including donors, non-governmental organizations (NGOs), and foreign publics, can view women's participation as a reflection of inclusive governance and a rejection of authoritarian structures, especially where insurgents fight against autocracies. As such, gender inclusion serves not only as a military or ideological asset but also as a low-cost tool to project democratic values, differentiate from rivals, and appeal to foreign allies. This was evident in the Syrian Civil War, where gender ideology became a key cleavage: groups that included women used this to signal democratic and progressive credentials to potential domestic and regional allies, while those that excluded women were associated with authoritarianism and linked to actors like the Assad regime or ISIS (Szekely, 2020).

Given that rebel groups often lack democratic structures like elections or checks and balances, cues such as gender inclusion may become especially salient; observers may rely on the presence of women in leadership or combat roles to infer a group's ideologies and post-conflict intentions. While how civilian treatment and international law alignment enhance rebel legitimacy is examined, the potential of female combatants to signal democratic alignment has not been explored. Examining whether women's participation conveys democratic values, even within rebel groups typically governed by hierarchical and authoritarian structures, offers a compelling test into the symbolic power of gender inclusion.

Gender equality is another value that can shape conflict assistance. Although the literature has yet to directly address gender equality as a factor in conflict assistance, related studies demonstrate that women's rights shape foreign aid trends (Dietrich et al., 2025) and public attitudes toward foreign actors. Countries that institutionalize political gender equality are considered more deserving of foreign aid (Bush and Zetterberg, 2021; Bush et al., 2024), and countries that rely on Western foreign aid, despite their questionable human rights records, are more willing to adopt gender quotas to signal their alignment with gender progressivism (Edgell, 2017).

A similar mechanism could likely work for gender-diverse groups, but is yet to be tested. Women's inclusion in rebel groups can make people think that their group embraces and fights for gender equality. While rebels typically do not mobilize around gender equality as a primary concern, first seeking rather to achieve greater autonomy or gain political and economic concessions, the presence of women fighters gives the groups a chance to frame their goals in a way that resonates with those concerned with women's rights. This can increase the organization's appeal in the eyes of international communities, especially those in liberal democracies. If people value gender equality, being gender-diverse would be more likely to earn groups a positive endorsement from the foreign public.

In sum, the presence of women in rebel groups can signal democratic values and gender equality, which can increase foreign public support for these groups. Although these groups are rarely democratic and rarely prioritize gender rights, gendered biases shape perceptions, helping observers interpret the conflict landscape. Media coverage and rebel outreach efforts further reinforce these associations, detailed next.

Media Coverage and Rebel Outreach: Media portrayal of female combatants can reinforce and reproduce their association with desirable ideologies and values, which can positively impact people's perceptions. Contemporary news coverage, especially from Western media outlets, tends to corroborate rebels' depiction of women as combating patriarchy (Nacos, 2005). News titles often refer to female militants as gender-equality advocates working toward emancipating suppressed women in their region. A title from *The Conversation* reads, "Colombian Militants Have a New Plan for the Country, and It's Called 'Insurgent Feminism'" (Boutron, 2017). Another one writes, "A 'Utopian' Society Promoting Gender Equality Continues to Rise from the Ashes of ISIS – Despite Turkish Attacks" and refers to Kurds' fight in Syria as a feminist revolution (Flock, 2024). Studies suggest that the media frames the female combatant as "exceptional, heroic, and one that deconstructs the masculinity of its adversary" (Toivanen and Baser, 2016). These depictions can help organizations with women fighters be perceived as righteous by international communities, especially those concerned with liberal democratic values, even when they use violence, which is disapproved of normatively.

Rebel groups' international outreach often aligns with media frames that emphasize women's involvement as a sign of gender equality and empowerment. Recruiting women helps project an inclusive image that appeals to both local and international audiences. For instance, although the Irish Republican Army (IRA) initially resisted women's participation, later pressures led to their inclusion to "demonstrate that the group represented a mass social movement" (Alison, 2004: 454). Similarly, FARC's recruitment of women fighters enhanced its image of inclusivity within Colombian communities (Herrera and Porch, 2008). The PKK underscores its commitment to gender equality by portraying women militants as the epitomes of democracy and freedom (PKK, 2023: 6). The YPJ (Women's Defense Units of the Kurdish insurgency in Syria - Yekineyen Parastina Jin, in Kurdish) drew international attention, with visits to Rojava from global committees, intellectuals, and politicians – including French President Hollande and Swedish Defense Minister Hultqvist. The US Central Command even highlighted the public interest in female fighters in a tweet featuring them (US Central Command, 2017b).

2.2.3 Instrumental Concerns

While the humanitarian and ideological heuristics associated with women can make people more supportive of assisting rebel groups when female combatants are visibly present, instrumental concerns can push the support in a different direction. Public support for rebel groups can hinge on strategic viability, namely their perceived likelihood of succeeding in a way that would advance their country's strategic interests. The presence of women in combat roles might signal military weakness, leading to decreased support. On the other hand, another instrumental factor, namely people's concern for their country's international reputation, may increase support for groups with female fighters, if people associate female fighters with pursuit of moral principles or gender equality.

First, concerns about the on-the-ground gains can reduce public support for gender-diverse rebel groups. People tend to back foreign interventions they see as likely to succeed (Eichenberg, 2005; Gelpi et al., 2009). Leaders also consider the probability of success when choosing to support armed groups, balancing this against potential security risks to their own country. The alignment between the group's effective operations and the security interests of the sponsoring state plays a crucial role, as states are reluctant to back groups that may inadvertently create long-term security vulnerabilities (Salehyan, Gleditsch, and Cunningham, 2011).

Women are erroneously perceived as deficient in the attributes that are essential for success in traditionally male domains (Heilman, 2001). Studies demonstrate that female politicians are not perceived as tough enough for 'masculinist" positions such as national security and foreign policy (Holman, Merolla, and Zechmeister, 2011; Lawless, 2004). These stereotypes persist in contemporary Western and non-Western contexts, with critical implications for women's actual political representation (Liu, 2018). Women are mainly assigned to more "feminine" cabinet positions (Krook and O'Brien, 2012) and are excluded from "masculine" positions, such as defense ministers during conflict, but are more likely to be appointed when the role becomes less conflict-centered (Barnes and O'Brien, 2018). As such, people can think that armed movements with women fighters are less likely to succeed.

Although skepticism about women's military capabilities has declined, some mainstream outlets continue to feature headlines such as "Women Do Not Belong in Combat" (Donald, 2019) and "Women Absolutely Do Not Belong in Combat" (Fischer, 2019), reflecting persistent conservative views. Recently, US Defense Minister Pete Hegseth argued against women in combat, claiming that it complicates fighting without improving effectiveness or lethality (NBC News, 2024). Similar debates appear internationally, as seen in headlines like "Female Frontline Soldiers Will Put Lives at Risk, Says Ex-Army Chief" (BBC, 2016) in the UK; "Israeli Army Debates Combat Roles for Women – With Rabbis Who Fiercely Oppose It" in Israel (Kubovich, 2021); and "Kuwait Allows Women to Join Military, Igniting Debate" (Amwaj Media, 2021). These negative perspectives toward women's military capacity can affect how people view their country's security gains if involved in the conflict. If people view women as less capable in combat, they may equate their presence with military weakness and be less inclined to support armed groups with female insurgents, as these groups might be perceived as posing a threat to the sponsoring state's security interests, ultimately reducing overall support.

Alternatively, people's instrumental concerns for increasing their country's reputation can increase support for gender-diverse groups if they associate women combatants with more righteous or gender-equal movements.

Leaders and the public value their country's reputation highly, often to the extent that decisions to use military force are driven by the desire to enhance or protect that reputation (Yarhi-Milo, 2018). Just as women's political representation can enhance an autocracy's international reputation, women in insurgency may serve a similar function, especially among foreign publics and decision-makers who are concerned with international reputation and view gender equality as an indication of status. This is because gender equality functions as a defining norm distinguishing states perceived as civilized and reputable from those deemed uncivilized and backward (Towns, 2010).

This reputational mechanism can be especially relevant in liberal democracies where foreign policy decisions are subject to public scrutiny and where alignment with women's rights is deemed to be both an ideological interest and a domestic expectation. For political elites, supporting a gender-diverse rebel group allows them to frame foreign involvement not just in terms of security but also as a status-enhancing commitment to advance gender equality. For citizens, backing such groups can bolster national prestige as it aligns their state with progressive values, elevating its reputation on the global stage as a promoter of gender equality. For instance, a recent piece in *Foreign Affairs* argues for America's continued hegemony in world affairs by upholding its reputation as a promoter of progressive values, and cites the alliance between the US and the SDF as an example of advancing democracy, human rights, and gender equality in the region (Stewart, Petkun, and Revkin, 2024). Sponsoring a movement led by women can be perceived as enhancing a country's reputation in the global community, potentially garnering stronger support for these groups than they would have if they lacked women.

To sum, I organize core factors that may affect foreign audiences' support for insurgencies in three groups, namely those focusing on: humanitarian concerns; ideologies and values; and sponsor interests. Mechanisms tied to audiences' humanitarian concerns and values lead to favorable assessments of rebels with women: these mechanisms amplify favorable perceptions regarding reduced violence, moral conduct, democratic principles, and gender equality. Mechanisms tied to instrumental concerns may lead to either positive or negative evaluations. Perception of women as lacking capability in conflict settings may lead to reduced support for rebels with women, due to perceptions of ineffectiveness in delivering gains for the sponsoring state on the ground, namely low success likelihood or jeopardizing security interests. Conversely, audiences may believe that sponsoring rebels with women positively influences their country's international reputation. I expect these mechanisms to impact foreign public opinions on lending foreign conflict assistance. I empirically test these expectations in the next section via original survey experiments.

3 Foreign Public Opinion toward Female Fighters: Experimental Analysis

Previous sections established that the gender composition of rebel groups can matter for public opinion and identified potential pathways through which this influence may operate. This section seeks to answer the following questions: Do foreign publics support armed movements featuring female fighters? How do they perceive these armed movements? Through what mechanisms does this support operate?

I also ask whether the perception of foreign armed movements varies systematically by citizens' gender or gender-egalitarian attitudes. This is important because the extant research shows that women and people with more gender-egalitarian attitudes are less supportive of use of force and conflict intervention abroad compared to men and people with more gender-unequal attitudes (Wood and Ramirez, 2018). This gender gap is deemed one of the most consistent findings in political psychology (Conover and Sapiro, 1993); however, whether such a gap exists when the perpetrators are female has not been tested. I use survey experiments to focus on the impact of women combatants, isolating other conflict-related factors that can influence people's support preferences, such as the country of origin or violence levels. I analyze these questions through survey experiments in the US and Tunisia.

3.1 Case Selection

The experiment is conducted over two samples: citizens of the US and of Tunisia. The US is the country engaging in foreign conflicts the most. It has a long history of providing various forms of assistance to rebel groups globally, ranging from involvement in Nicaragua, Cuba, Angola, and Iran during the Cold War, to interventions following the "global war on terror" policy in Libya and Afghanistan, to more recent engagements in Syria. These actions often sparked debates within domestic politics, where the opposition and the public have questioned the appropriateness and the consequences of supporting or terminating aid to various groups. Hence, understanding US attitudes on support for foreign conflicts is crucial in its own right and can also offer insights into the perspectives of other democratic audiences across Western nations.

Tunisia offers a valuable case with which to test the generalizability of the findings. On the one hand, like the US, Tunisia has been recognized as a democracy, hence we would expect public opinion to shape policymaking,

making it a relevant comparison. The first free and fair elections were held in 2011 after Arab Spring, and a new constitution adopted in 2014 solidified the democratic framework. Tunisia was the only Arab nation classified as "free" in the 2020 Freedom House Index and was often referred to as "a democratic success story." However, since 2021 Tunisia has been downgraded to "partially free" by Freedom House and reclassified from a "liberal democracy" to an "electoral autocracy" in V-Dem, as President Said curbed the powers of the parliament and the judiciary. This democratic backsliding raises questions about the extent to which public opinion shapes policymaking. Nonetheless, hybrid regimes like Tunisia, where democratic and authoritarian elements coexist, provide an opportunity to examine how public opinion functions within constrained democratic settings. Analyzing Tunisia helps me assess whether the findings apply beyond liberal democracies and to discuss public opinion's role under conditions of increasing executive dominance.

In both Tunisia and the US, women constitute 16–17 percent of their state's militaries (US Department of Defense, 2022; US Embassy in Tunisia, 2021), suggesting a similarity in people's familiarity with women's involvement in more masculine domains. On the other hand, Tunisia differs from the US in important ways, notably regarding military power and historical involvement in foreign conflicts, the strength of traditional gender norms, exposure to conflict, and the portrayal of female fighters in mainstream news media. These differences may lead to different attitudes toward gender-diverse groups and conflict assistance in general, representing potential challenges for the mechanisms underlined in Section 3. These make the Tunisian case informative about the extent to which the theorized mechanisms travel across contexts.

Particularly, the US has a more formally educated and high-income population where gender-progressive informal and formal institutions are more accepted, while the Tunisian population is generally more conservative. I expect that the strength of traditional gender stereotypes would be greater in Tunisia, providing a good case to test whether women's involvement in combat creates backlashes. Further, audiences experiencing conflict in their own home country may be more hesitant to support sending conflict assistance abroad as they are more familiar with the devastating consequences of such aid. Tunisia experienced more internal conflict (such as al-Qaeda in the Islamic Maghreb [AQIM] and the Islamic State–linked Jund al-Khilafah-Tunisia [JAK-T]). The US, on the other hand, while facing terrorist attacks (9/11) and intervening in Afghanistan and Iraq, has not faced persistent internal insurgencies involving organized rebel groups within its borders in recent decades.

Moreover, the salience of female fighters in the mainstream media differs significantly for the US and Tunisia. The US supported the YPG (People's Defense Units – Yekîneyên Parastina Gel, in Kurdish) against ISIS in Syria and Iraq. Numerous news stories featuring the Kurdish female fighters of the YPJ – an all-female brigade of the YPG – circulated in the US, depicting them as feminist heroines and the carriers of Western secular ideals against the radical Islamist agenda of ISIS, praising their bravery and military prowess (Yesiltas, 2022). For instance, a *New York Times* article title read "Women Fight ISIS and Sexism in Kurdish Regions" (Flanagin, 2014). This gender dichotomy between 'empowered YPJ' versus 'subjugated ISIS women' dominated Western coverage of the Syrian war (Sjoberg, 2018).

On the other hand, in the Tunisian media, female fighters have remained largely invisible; when they are mentioned, it is typically in a negative context. A keyword search involving phrases such as "female fighters, female insurgent, female terrorist, female jihadist, rebels, insurgents, jihadist" from the two most read newspapers in Tunisia – Al Chourouk and La Presse – between 2013 and 2023 yielded forty-six news articles, only thirteen of which focus specifically on female fighters. Most of those forty-six articles focus on the so-called sexual jihad (appearing thirty-eight times), which refers to noncombatant women joining ISIS to provide sexual labor to ISIS men; women are depicted in a very negative frame, condemning their radicalization. Only one article offers a positive portrayal, depicting an Iraqi woman as a symbol of resistance who kills an ISIS leader in revenge after being subjected to "sexual jihad" (Al Chourouk, 2015). Overall, given all these differences, Tunisia provides a useful case for addressing these potential differences and testing arguments' generalization beyond Western states.

3.2 Survey Experiment Design

I conducted online survey experiments with citizens. Various international audiences can be relevant for rebel groups aiming to conduct public outreach, build reputable images, and attract foreign support, such as international media and journalists, NGOs, international organizations, foreign governments (including politicians, bureaucrats, diplomats), diaspora communities and advocacy groups (including anti-war organizations, peace movements, human rights groups), academic institutions and think tanks, crowdfunding platforms, public figures, and citizens. Due to the breadth of the appropriate sample and for practicality, I conducted survey experiments with citizens. The literature on foreign conflict assistance typically focuses on citizens' opinions as they influence government policies, media narratives, and international support for these groups (Kertzer and Zeitzoff, 2017).

I recruited 840 US participants via AmazonTurk and 927 Tunisian participants via TGM Research in March–June 2024. The Tunisian sample compares well with census data on key dimensions, such as gender, education, and age. The US sample is slightly tilted toward males and more Democrat-leaning, as with most online surveys, but aligns well with census data on key factors (Table A1). Experimental research often uses AmazonTurk samples, and various studies have agreed on their reliability (Clifford, Jewell, and Waggoner, 2015).

The experiments involved the same questions in both samples. At the beginning, participants completed a standard battery of demographic questions, followed by a brief questionnaire measuring their gender-equality attitudes, opinions on whether the US/Tunisia should take an active role in world affairs, and news consumption habits. These factors are relevant to the research questions as gender attitudes are expected to influence support for gender-diverse movements, and those who believe that their governments should be active internationally are likely to have stronger opinions on foreign interventions. News consumption measures their interest in foreign policy and exposure to female fighters in the mainstream media.

The respondents were then asked to consider a hypothetical scenario that their country could face in the future, one that is general and not about a real country or group in the news today. Respondents were randomly assigned to either a "female combatant" or a "male combatant" treatment (the control group). Those in the "female combatant treatment" saw news items featuring female fighters, while the control group saw identical scenarios with male fighters (Figure 1). Each treatment included images and a background story for the insurgency, designed as news items in a newspaper, helping respondents visualize the conflict as a situation likely to happen. The photos were chosen for their similarity: combatants holding guns upward among other combatants, likely in military training.[5] Everything in the treatments was the same except for the photo of the insurgents (see Appendix for the survey instrument). The experiment reflects a low-information environment, which typically characterizes the public's understanding of conflicts abroad. The design deliberately excludes the usual positive portrayals of female combatants in media and

---

[5] Photos of Kurdish YPG and YPJ fighters from the Syrian Civil War were used because it was easier to find similar images of male and female insurgents, and real photographs are used to simulate an authentic newspaper layout. This detail was not shared with respondents; they were informed that the scenario was not about a specific insurgency, assuming that foreign audiences wouldn't identify Kurdish rebels. An open-ended question at the end of the survey asking respondents if they could identify which group the photos represented confirmed this assumption. Only 2.26 percent guessed Kurdish rebels in the US sample (19 in 840), and 0.97 percent in the Tunisian sample (9 in 927), making no meaningful effect on the results.

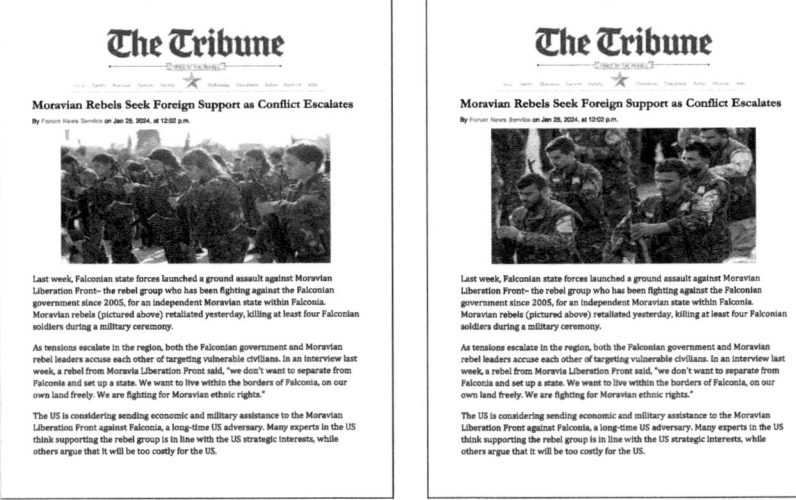

Figure 1 Treatments.[6]

rebel narratives, discussed in Sections 2 and 3, to isolate female fighters' impact on support, hence presents a hard case to find a treatment effect.

The news item includes information about a fictitious rebel group fighting against a similarly fictitious US/Tunisian adversary state, asking for support from the US/Tunisia. Brutger et al. (2023) show that using hypothetical scenarios with fictional actors does not change results compared to real scenarios, supporting the reliability of this approach. The vignette for both treatments is as follows:

> Last week, Falconian state forces launched a ground assault against Moravian Liberation Front – the rebel group who has been fighting against the Falconian government since 2005, for an independent Moravian state within Falconia. Moravian rebels (pictured above) retaliated yesterday, killing at least four Falconian soldiers during a military ceremony. As tensions escalate in the region, both the Falconian government and Moravian rebel leaders accuse each other of targeting vulnerable civilians. In an interview last week, a rebel from Moravia Liberation Front said, "We do not want to separate from Falconia and set up a state. We want to live within the borders of Falconia, on our own land freely. We are fighting for Moravian ethnic rights." The US/Tunisia is considering sending economic and military assistance to the Moravian Liberation Front against Falconia, a long-time US/Tunisia

---

[6] The format of the newspapers is inspired by Clayton et al. (2019). See Figures A2.1, A.2.2, A2.3, and A2.4 in the Appendix for Arabic versions and larger/full versions. Photo credits: Delil Souleiman/AFP via Getty Images.

adversary. Many experts in the US/Tunisia think supporting the rebel group is in line with the US/Tunisian strategic interests, while others argue that it will be too costly for the US/Tunisia.

Participants were asked to answer a series of questions capturing their attitudes toward the potential US/Tunisian sponsorship of the armed group (*outcome measures*), and their perceptions of the armed group. Questions in the latter category measure the characteristics attributed to insurgent groups upon seeing the gender of the combatants. How people perceive groups based on the gender of the cadre is interesting and important in its own right, but I am also interested in seeing whether and to what extent these beliefs about women insurgents influence support for conflict assistance, hence I refer to them as *mediators* in the rest of the study. Chaudoin, Gaines, and Livny (2021) show that the order of mediators and outcome measures can be consequential for the mediation analysis results. Hence, I randomized the sequence in which the mediator and outcome variables appeared to ensure reliable results. To prevent the order of questions from influencing responses, I separately randomized the sequence of outcome measures and the sequence of mediators within their respective groups as well.

There are four outcome variables to capture the variation in different support types: (1) verbal endorsement, (2) economic support, (3) military intervention, (4) accepting refugees. Examining these distinct support types offers insight into how the presence of female combatants might influence different forms of aid. Verbal endorsement, being the least costly, is likely most sensitive to their inclusion, while costly options like military intervention may be less affected. Refugee acceptance further reveals attitudes toward the broader conflict environment, as it involves humanitarian considerations beyond direct support for the insurgents. Also, in refugee contexts, vulnerability is often portrayed through a gendered lens, with images of women and children symbolizing helplessness and tragedy, usually biasing public opinion against male refugees (Kreft and Agerberg, 2024). Female combatant treatment challenges this "feminization of vulnerability," likely juxtaposing women's agency in violence with common portrayals of victimhood, making it noteworthy to assess their influence on refugee acceptance attitudes. These outcomes are assessed by asking respondents to indicate how strongly they agree or disagree with the respective statements: The US/Tunisia should (1) verbally endorse the Moravian insurgent group, (2) provide economic support to the Moravian insurgent group, (3) militarily intervene on behalf of the Moravian insurgent group, (4) accept 500 refugees from the conflict hotspot. Each outcome is modeled as a separate dependent variable and analyzed using ordinary least squares (OLS) regression for US and Tunisian respondents independently.

Moreover, respondents were asked to evaluate the rebel group, through questions such as "In your opinion, to what extent does the Moravian insurgent group use violence against civilians; embrace democratic/gender-equal attitudes; [follow a] tactic of armed struggle [that] is morally justified; [and to what extent would] supporting the Moravian insurgency ... be good for the security interests of the US/Tunisia?" (see Appendix for the survey instrument). All questions are measured on a five-point scale, from 1 = strongly disagree to 5 = strongly agree. Again, each question is modeled separately, with US and Tunisian respondents analyzed independently, using OLS regression.

3.3 Results

Do female combatants increase foreign support for sponsoring their groups? Figures 2 and 3 present the main results for the US and Tunisian samples, respectively. I present results without controls in the main text and those with controls (such as age, gender, education, US activity, ideology, news following, and gender attitudes) in the Appendix. Overall, results show that seeing female combatants increases people's support for foreign insurgencies compared to seeing male combatants.

For the US sample, results indicate that the presence of female combatants significantly increases verbal endorsement of the conflict, with an average treatment effect (ATE) of 0.24 (and 0.28 with control variables), which is statistically significant at the 0.01 level (Table A2, Appendix). Similarly, for economic support, the presence of female combatants shows a positive but weaker impact, with a statistically significant effect only when control variables are included (0.13 at $p < 0.05$). Likewise, the presence of female combatants has a positive and significant effect on accepting refugees from the conflict region (0.15, $p < 0.1$). That said, there is no significant effect on support for military intervention on behalf of the insurgency, with coefficients close to zero. These results suggest that the presence of female combatants substantively and significantly increases public support for the rebel groups, particularly in areas of verbal endorsement, economic support, and refugee acceptance for American citizens.

The effect sizes are relatively large. The support for verbally endorsing a foreign rebel group increases by 11–13 percent when women insurgents are visibly present compared to the support levels for male combatants.[7] To put it

---

[7] Calculated by dividing the coefficients of increased support with and without controls (0.28 and 0.24) by the support that male combatants received on a five-point Likert scale (0.21), adjusted to a 0–4 scale (from lowest to highest support).

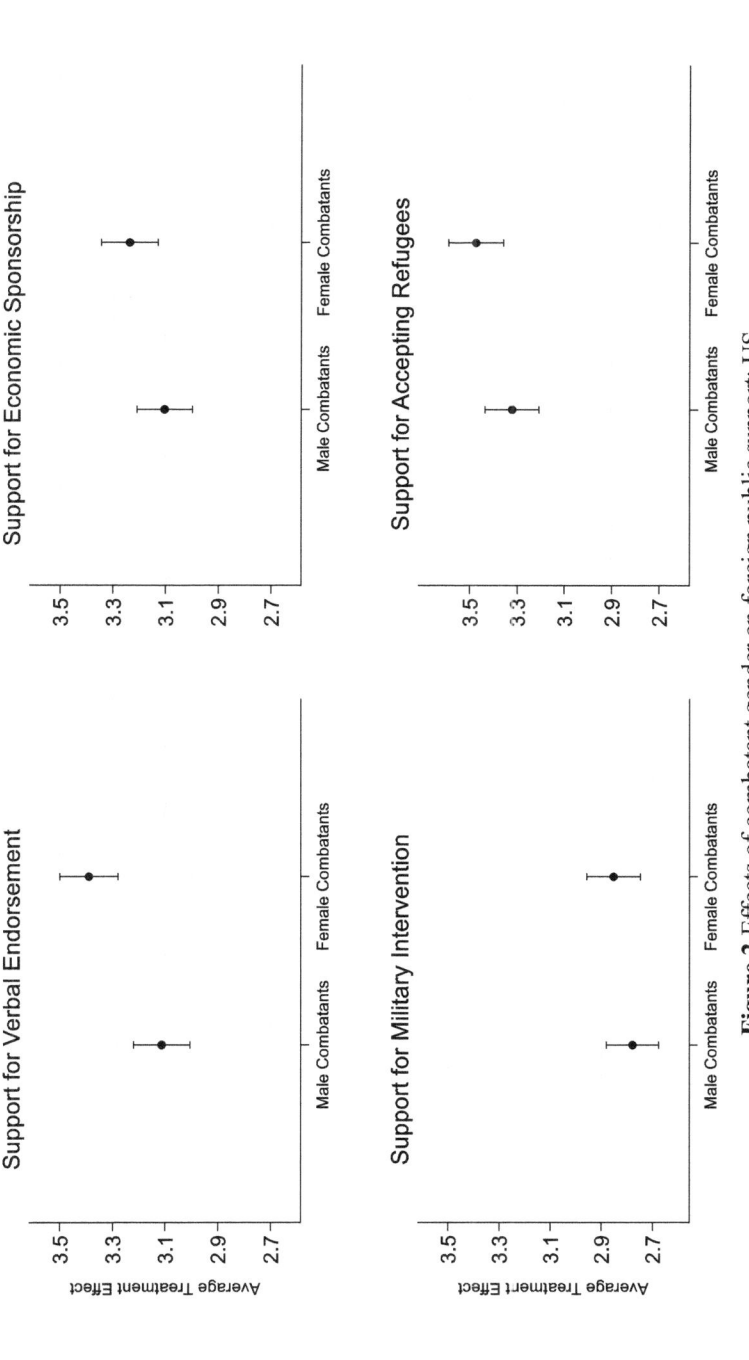

Figure 2 Effects of combatant gender on foreign public support: US.

Note: The figure represents average support levels by treatments based on Table A2 (Models 1, 3, 5, 7 without controls) in the US sample. Lines represent 95 percent confidence intervals. Dependent variables are measured on a five-point scale, with higher numbers indicating greater approval. Average treatment effects (ATEs) are statistically significant for verbal endorsement ($p < 0.01$), refugee acceptance ($p < 0.1$) [and economic support when control variables are included ($p < 0.1$, Model 4)], but not for military intervention.

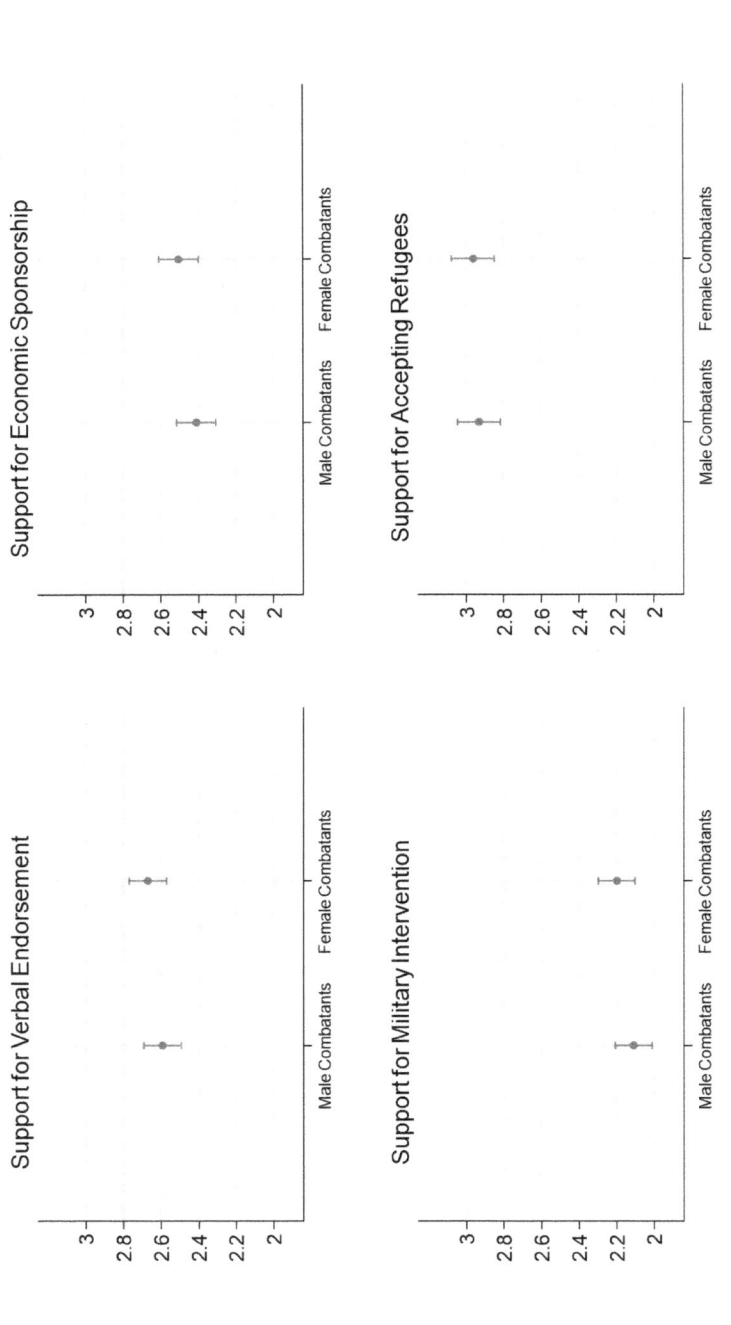

Figure 3 Effects of combatant gender on foreign public support: Tunisia.

Note: The figure represents average Tunisian support levels by treatments based on Table A3 (Models 1, 3, 5, 7 without controls). Lines represent 95 percent confidence intervals. Dependent variables are measured on a five-point scale, with higher numbers indicating greater approval. Average treatment effects are not statistically significant at conventional significance levels.

into perspective, this effect is four to five times greater than the effect that political ideology has in supporting US sponsorship (see Model 2 in Table A2 in the Appendix). Also, this effect size is slightly higher than the public's reluctance to support military strikes against democratic countries compared to autocracies in Tomz and Weeks' (2013) seminal article (often considered a key empirical foundation of the democratic peace thesis).

The Tunisian sample's results are parallel to those of the US sample. Overall, seeing female combatants increases support for the rebel group in all four support domains; however, the change in support levels is much smaller, and none of the support indicators are statistically significant (Figure 3). Verbal endorsement, economic sponsorship, support for military intervention, and accepting refugees all show slight increases with ATEs of 0.08, 0.09, 0.09, and 0.03, respectively, but these are substantively small and not significant at traditionally accepted levels (Table A3 in the Appendix). The average agreeableness on any type of support for a conflict abroad is notably lower than that of the US sample, for both male and female combatants. For instance, favoring verbal endorsement for female combatants in the US sample is approximately 30 percent higher than in the Tunisian sample.

This difference between US and Tunisian samples can be related to the factors outlined in Section 3.1, namely low exposure to female combatants in the news items and less propensity to view getting involved in foreign conflict as legitimate, as reflected in their historical foreign policy trends. While support for women combatants is not statistically significant compared to support for male combatants in Tunisia, there is no backlash toward them either.

3.3.1 Heterogeneous Treatment Effects: How Do Respondent Gender and Gender Attitudes Affect Support?

Support for armed groups increases among both men and women when female combatants are involved, with similar response magnitudes. In the US, male respondents' support for verbal endorsement rises from 3.28 for male combatants to 3.48 for female combatants, while female respondents' support increases from 2.90 to 3.16 (Figure 4). Although female respondents show significantly lower baseline support levels across all support types, this gendered effect disappears when we control for other factors such as age, education, ideology, foreign policy attitudes, and gender attitudes (Table A4). Also, women demonstrate a substantive increase in endorsement for female combatants, bringing their support levels closer to those of male respondents (with a 0.2 point increase among male respondents, and 0.26 among female respondents). The nonsignificant interaction terms confirm that both genders react similarly to the

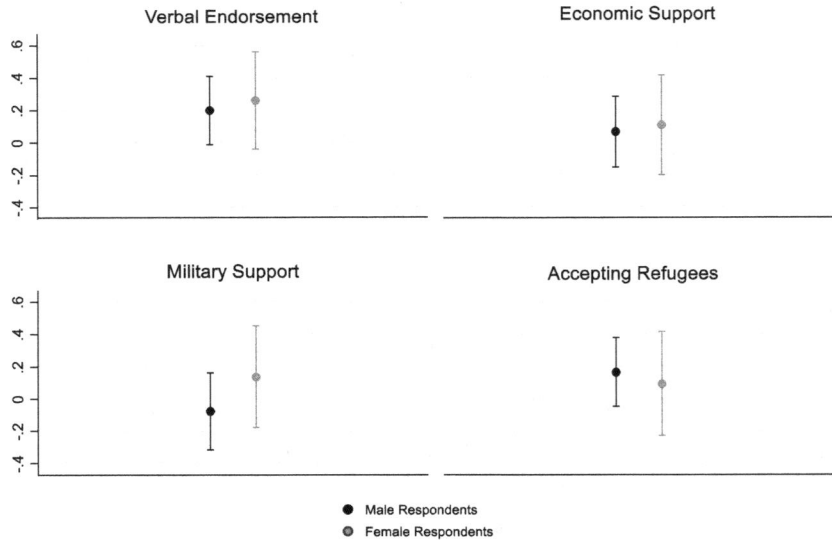

Figure 4 Heterogeneous treatment effects by respondent gender: US.
Note: The figure represents ATEs on different support types across respondent genders in the US sample, based on Table A4 (Models 1, 3, 5, 7 without controls). Lines represent 95 percent confidence intervals. Dependent variables are measured on a five-point scale, with higher values indicating greater approval. Interactions between respondent gender and the treatment are not statistically significant at conventional levels.

presence of female combatants across types of support, indicating no substantial gender-based difference in supporting female combatants.

Both genders generally react similarly to the presence of female combatants in terms of economic support and acceptance of refugees. However, the presence of female combatants slightly decreases support for military intervention among American male respondents (by −0.08) and slightly increases support among female respondents (by 0.14), albeit this is not statistically significant. Nevertheless, the decrease among men may suggest a potential aversion to military intervention when female combatants are involved. Otherwise, the consistent positive direction suggests a general trend toward higher overall support of both female and male respondents when female combatants are involved.

The results are interesting because the change in support levels upon seeing female combatants is slightly higher among female respondents (except for refugee acceptance) than male respondents. These results contribute to the scholarship finding a consistent gender gap in support of the use of force: In line with the literature, women's baseline support levels for the insurgency are lower, yet this gap disappears when controls are included. Also, contrary to this scholarship, when women are the combatants, female support for conflict assistance rises in a way that is parallel to how male support levels rise. Social identity theory may explain this; people favor in-groups over out-groups. This deserves attention as gender is not typically considered among the social identity categories shaping conflict support. Future research can explore whether this reflects gender solidarity or holds across different contexts.

The Tunisian sample shows similar results regarding female respondents' receptiveness to supporting female combatants (Figure 5). The effect of seeing female versus male combatants does not vary significantly between male and female respondents. In other words, both male and female respondents react similarly to the presence of female combatants across the support types, with no evidence of a gendered difference in response to female combatants, except for refugee support, where women show lower support overall. Notably, unlike in the US, Tunisian women do not show significantly lower baseline support for

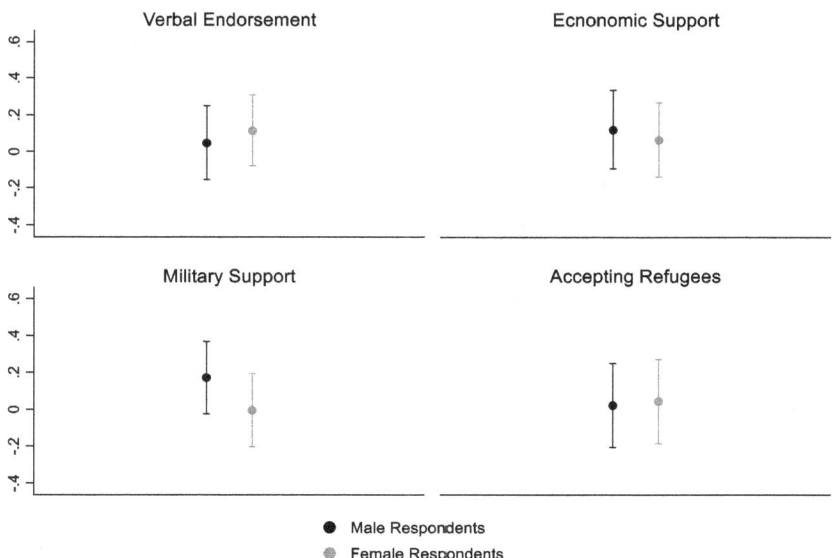

Figure 5 Heterogeneous treatment effects by respondent gender: Tunisia.
Note: The figure represents ATEs on different support types across respondent genders in the Tunisian sample, based on Table A5 (Models 1, 3, 5, 7 without controls). Lines represent 95 percent confidence intervals. Dependent variables are measured on a five-point scale, with higher values indicating greater approval. Interactions between respondent gender and the treatment are not statistically significant at conventional levels.

sponsoring groups abroad, challenging the expectations of the women–peace hypothesis.

Additionally, the presence of female combatants leads to a significant increase in Tunisian males' support for military intervention (0.17, p < 0.1, with an even stronger effect when control variables are considered, see Table A5). This finding is intriguing as it contrasts with the American men's decreased support for female combatants. It also counters the expectations of a conservative backlash, which might suggest instead that norms around protecting women may drive increased willingness among men to support military intervention when female combatants are involved.

How do individual attitudes toward gender equality impact support for female combatants? Do conservative audiences disapprove of female combatants abandoning traditional gender roles, leading them to withhold support? Figures 6 and 7 display Americans' and Tunisians' support levels by their average gender-egalitarian attitudes, respectively. I measure gender-egalitarian attitudes by asking respondents to what extent they agree with the statement "In general, men are more fit than women to be political leaders." I measure gender-egalitarian attitudes prior to the treatments: 1 denotes the most gender equal and 5 the most gender unequal attitudes.

The results indicate that while gender attitudes do not lead Americans to evaluate female combatants differently than male combatants, individuals with stronger gender-unequal attitudes show significantly increased support for overall insurgency (for both female and male combatants) for all support types except refugee acceptance. This effect is statistically significant (p < 0.01), substantively large (0.2 and 0.4-point increase for verbal and for economic and military support, respectively), and robust, even accounting for factors like age, gender, education, political ideology, foreign policy attitudes, and news consumption patterns.

The Tunisian results differ from those of the US (Figure 7). Gender attitudes are not statistically related to Tunisians' support levels for the overall insurgency. However, individuals with more unequal attitudes tend to show higher economic and military support for groups with female combatants (unlike the US). While the presence of female combatants decreases economic and military support among those with highest gender-egalitarian attitudes, support levels increase among those with stronger traditional gender perspectives by 0.15–0.16 points (Models 3, 5, 6 in Table A7).

This result defies expectations of a conservative backlash; individuals with the most gender-unequal attitudes – those who generally oppose women's public roles – show greater support for women who step away from traditional gender roles by joining a rebel group. On the other hand, those who embrace more gender-progressive attitudes, those who have normalized women's public

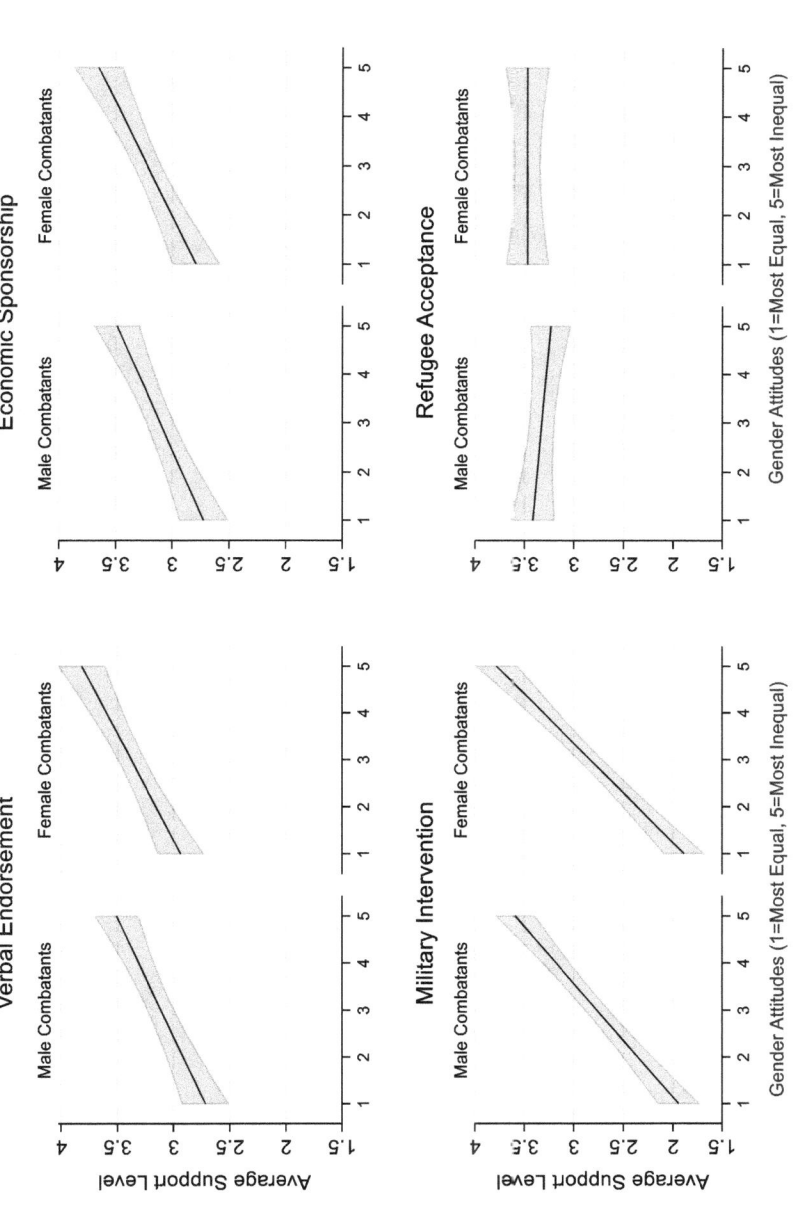

Figure 6 Heterogenous treatment effects by respondent gender attitudes: US.

Note: The figure represents average support levels on different support types across respondent gender attitudes in the US sample, based on Table A6 (Models 1, 3, 5, 7 without controls). Lines represent 95 percent confidence intervals. Dependent variables are measured on a five-point scale, with higher values indicating greater approval. Interactions between respondent gender attitudes and the treatment are not statistically significant at conventional levels.

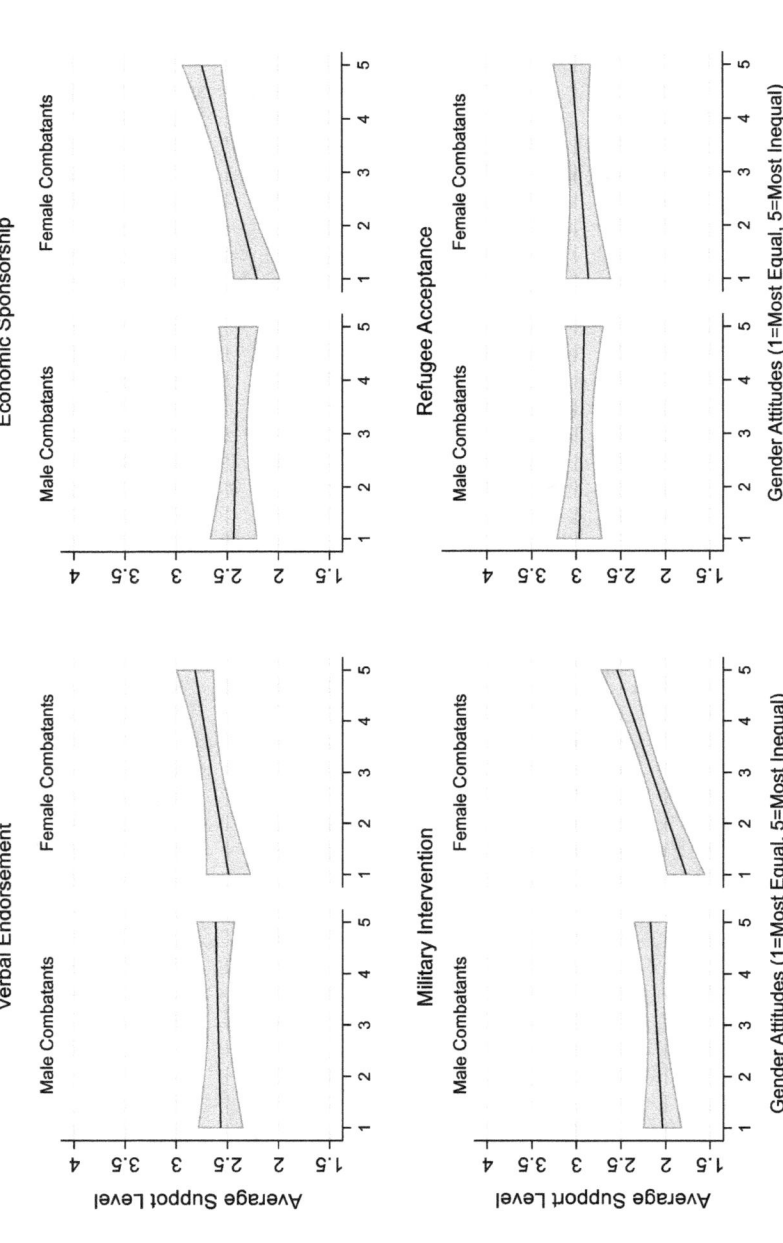

Figure 7 Heterogenous treatment effects by respondent gender attitudes: Tunisia.

Note: The figure represents average support levels on different support types across respondent gender attitudes in the Tunisian sample, based on Table A7 (Models 1, 3, 5, 7 without controls). Lines represent 95 percent confidence intervals. Dependent variables are measured on a five-point scale, with higher values indicating greater approval. Interactions between respondent gender attitudes and the treatment are statistically significant for economic sponsorship ($p < 0.05$) and military intervention ($p < 0.01$).

participation, show little change in support when women are fighting in a conflict. This finding highlights a previously overlooked interaction between gender attitudes and the gender of perpetrators in conflict, discussed further in the conclusion, Section 5.

3.3.2 How Do Foreign Audiences Perceive Armed Groups with Female Combatants?

The results so far indicate that the gender composition of armed groups significantly shapes the level of support that foreign publics deem appropriate. Then, do foreign publics apply different standards to groups with female combatants? Do they believe that women fighters' presence is a sign of a moral or feminist cause, or do foreign audiences focus on the potential strategic benefits instead, such as enhancing their country's reputation? How does the inclusion of female fighters influence the foreign publics' perceptions of these groups? Here, I examine the direct effects of the mechanisms outlined in Section 2.2, focusing on how the presence of female combatants shapes perceptions of rebel groups. Specifically, I explore three dimensions: their humanitarian character, assessed through perceptions of (1) the group's use of civilian violence, (2) its moral justification of its armed tactics, and (3) the level of repression it faces; the group's ideologies and values, evaluated through (4) its commitment to democratic principles and (5) gender equality; and instrumental concerns for the sponsoring state, including (6) the group's military capacity and (7) its ability to enhance the state's security and (8) reputation.

The findings, drawn from both American and Tunisian samples, indicate that the presence of women insurgents generally has a largely positive impact on rebel groups' image. Contrary to expectations, there is no significant indication that the group is perceived as weaker when women are involved. Instead, when people see women combatants, they assume that the insurgency is more committed to democracy and gender-egalitarian values – this is the most profound impact of female combatants in both countries. They also change foreign audiences' opinions on the organization's armed tactics: When women are present, armed groups' tactics are considered more moral (in both countries) and less likely to be viewed as attacking civilians (especially in the US sample).

I begin by detailing the US results. Figure 8 shows that the perception that the group is egalitarian increases by 0.61 points when women are involved. This increase is more than half a point on a five-point scale, statistically significant and robust to model variations, suggesting that the presence of women combatants is strongly associated with viewing armed groups as promoting gender equality. Second, the presence of female combatants significantly increases the

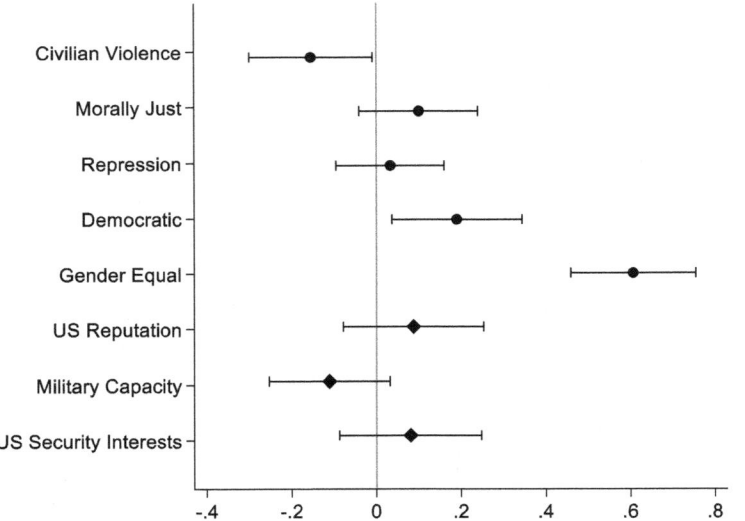

Figure 8 How are groups with female combatants perceived in the US?
Note: The figure represents ATEs of opinions toward rebel group characteristics and sponsor interests in the US sample, based on Table A8 (Models 1, 3, 5, 7, 9, 11, 13, 15 without controls). Lines represent 95 percent confidence intervals. Dependent variables are measured on a five-point scale, with higher values indicating higher evaluations.

perception that the armed organization embraces democratic principles. The perception that the organization is democratic increases by 0.19 points (and 0.23 points with control variables), suggesting that individuals view groups with female combatants as more inclusive and representative of democratic ideals (Table A8 in the Appendix).

Female combatants also make a difference regarding the humanitarian appeal of these groups. When women are involved, people are less likely to think that the organization attacks civilians. Female combatants are associated with a statistically significant reduction in perceived civilian violence by around 0.15 points (p < 0.01). This implies a modest but notable shift in public perception toward viewing these groups as less violent toward civilians. Female combatants enhance the image of the armed groups as inclusive, progressive, and less violent.

Similarly, female combatants enhance the perception that the organization is morally just by 0.13 points, which is significant at p < 0.1 only when control variables are involved. Further, the visible presence of female combatants can lead people to think that supporting the organization is good for the reputation of the sponsoring state. Compared to males, female combatants lead to a minor positive change, 0.13 points (significant at $p < 0.1$ only when control variables are included, Table A8). Although the change is small, it suggests that the involvement of female combatants may enhance perceptions of the strategic reputation of the US, potentially making its involvement in armed conflicts appear more favorable.

While female combatants are viewed as militarily weaker than male combatants, this effect is minor and not statistically significant. When asked if supporting the group helps US security interests, there is a minor positive effect that is not statistically significant. Similarly, there is no evidence for the prevalence of the thinking that the conditions must be so severe that even women are fighting. The presence of female combatants does not seem to affect how people view the repression levels in the conflict region.

Overall, the results show that the presence of female combatants significantly enhances the image of the armed groups, especially in terms of reinforcing values of egalitarianism, democracy, as well as restraint in violence against civilians. The visible presence of female combatants leads to modest increases in perceptions that the organization pursues morally just strategies and that supporting the insurgency could enhance the US' reputation.

The results from Tunisia are very similar to those of the US (Figure 9). Tunisians also view the values and tactics of rebel groups more favorably when women are involved, suggesting external validity and the robustness of the results across different audiences with varying levels of gender norms and conflict exposure.

Similar to the US sample, Tunisians think that groups with female combatants are more democratic and gender-equal, by 0.17 points ($p < 0.05$) and by 0.24 points ($p < 0.01$), respectively. Moreover, upon seeing women combatant photos, Tunisians are significantly more likely to think that the organization is pursuing a more moral fight, by 0.14 points compared to those who saw male fighter photos ($p < 0.1$). The results are statistically significant both with and without control variables.

Other dimensions are not statistically significant but are noteworthy as they defy expectations in not showing negative perceptions toward women insurgents. There is no sign of backlash for sponsoring supporting female fighters or underestimating the military strength of female combatants; on the contrary, groups with female combatants are evaluated in a positive light on all grounds in Tunisia as well (more so than in the US, for instance, in terms of military capacity). Also, female combatants give the impression that the group attacks civilians less than all-male groups (0.11). Taken together, the results suggest that female combatants improve the inclusivity and the humanitarian image of

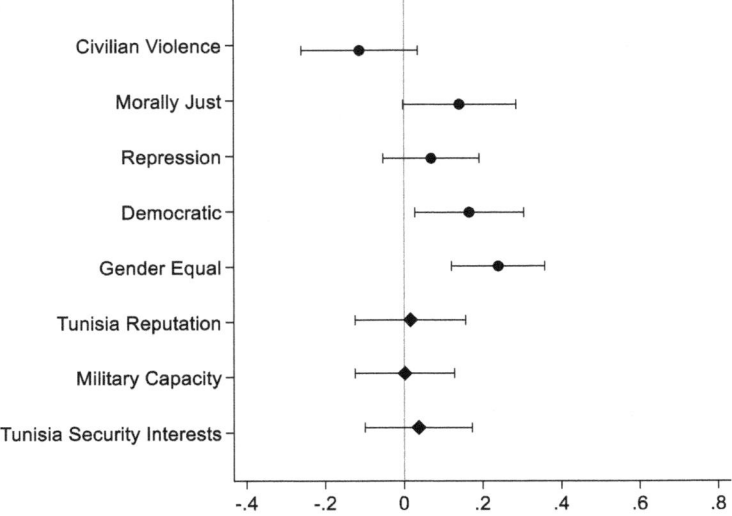

Figure 9 How are groups with female combatants perceived in Tunisia?
Note: The figure represents ATEs of opinions toward rebel group characteristics and sponsor interests in the Tunisian sample, based on Table A9 (Models 1, 3, 5, 7, 9, 11, 13, 15 without controls). Lines represent 95 per cent confidence intervals. Dependent variables are measured on a five-point scale, with higher values indicating higher evaluations.

armed groups, regardless of their actual deeds, which attests to their symbolic power in marketing the rebellion to international audiences and patrons.

3.3.3 Causal Mediation Analysis

In this last step of the experimental analysis, I examine whether the shifts in beliefs identified in Section 3.3.2 are important mechanisms through which the treatments affect preferences for lending support to foreign armed groups. I use causal mediation analysis to illustrate whether these beliefs associated with female combatants mediate the relationship between the experimental treatment and support for sponsoring their armed groups. I use the approach described by Imai et al. (2011) to estimate the treatment effect on each potential mediator and the effect of the mediator on support for intervention, where the estimates are then used to compute the average causal mediation effect. This framework helps differentiate between alternative mechanisms to calculate how much of the treatment effect travels through each mediating variable. The "total effect" comprises two components: the "indirect effect," which refers to the effect traveling through the mediator variable, and the "direct effect," referring to

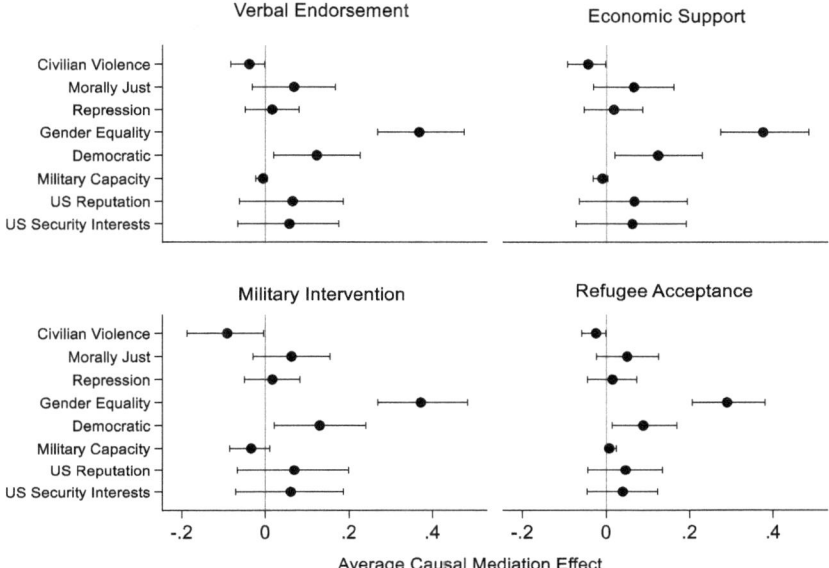

Figure 10 Causal mediation analysis: US.

Note: The figure represents the effect of the treatment on support levels mediated through each mechanism in the US sample. Mediation analysis was conducted individually on each mediator using Hicks and Tingley (2011). Lines represent 95 percent confidence intervals. Models are estimated by OLS regression.

the remaining effect of all the other possible channels (Imai et al., 2011). For each mediator, Monte Carlo simulations are used to estimate the effect of the treatment mediated by the proposed mediator variables, allowing for flexible modeling at every stage of estimation, as opposed to, for instance, classical structural equation estimation.

Figure 10 presents the results of the causal mediation analysis for the US, which are based on separate models for each mediator variable. The results show that potential mediators are correlated with the outcome support variables in the expected direction. An exception is the US security interests: I have hypothesized that female combatants would decline support for the insurgency as people would think that siding with females in a conflict may hurt their strategic interests; however, female combatants, again, are thought to improve the strategic interests of the sponsoring state. Another exception is the perception of civilian violence, discussed later. Overall, there are no meaningful differences across the outcome variables; across all four support categories – verbal endorsement, economic support, military intervention, and refugee acceptance – three mediators consistently stand out as statistically significant: gender equality, democracy, and civilian violence.

The perception that the group with female combatants embraces gender equality accounts for the largest mediated effect of support among other mediators, across all four support categories. Seeing women as combatants increases support for verbal, economic, and military backing of the insurgency by around 0.37, and increases accepting refugees from the conflict zone by 0.3 points through the mediated effect of the insurgency's perceived gender equality ($p < 0.01$).[8] Similarly, seeing women combatants increases supporting the insurgency verbally, economically, and militarily by around 0.13 points through the mediated effect of the insurgency's perceived embracing of democratic ideals,[9] and accepting refugees by 0.09 points ($p < 0.01$). These results are noteworthy because female combatants on their own did not directly influence people's support for military intervention (as reported in Figure 8), but when people perceive that these groups advocate for women's rights and democratic values, they are in favor of intervening in the conflict even militarily on behalf of these groups.

The indirect effects of civilian violence are negative in the US sample, differing from the expectations. While the presence of female combatants leads to the perception that the rebel group uses less civilian violence (as in Figure 8), the mediated effect through this perception is negative, as people express lower support for the group.[10] This might be related to associating a reduction in civilian violence with weakness or ineffectiveness of the group (compared to perhaps more aggressive all-male groups), making them less inclined to support, despite the overall positive moral signal of reduced civilian violence. Indeed, American citizens think that the group with female combatants is militarily weaker compared to the male combatants by −0.11 (albeit not reaching statistical significance: Figures 8 and 10, and Tables A8 and A10 in the Appendix). Importantly, the negative mediated effect of civilian violence is driven by male respondents; female respondents' support levels are not affected by perceptions of civilian violence (see Figure A2 in the Appendix). Other potential mechanisms, such as an increased concern for government repression,

---

[8] The perception of gender equality has a large positive indirect effect on the outcome variables, while its direct effect is negative. This suggests that the positive influence of female combatants largely depends on the perception that their group supports gender equality; without this perception, the presence of female combatants might reduce support due to other negative factors.

[9] Verbal endorsement: 0.123, $p < 0.01$; economic support: 0.124, $p < 0.01$; military intervention: 0.130, $p < 0.001$

[10] The mediation analysis reveals a decline in verbal endorsement (−0.04, $p < 0.05$), support for economic aid (−0.04, $p < 0.01$), and military intervention (−0.09, $p < 0.01$), contrary to the expectation that reduced violence would increase support.

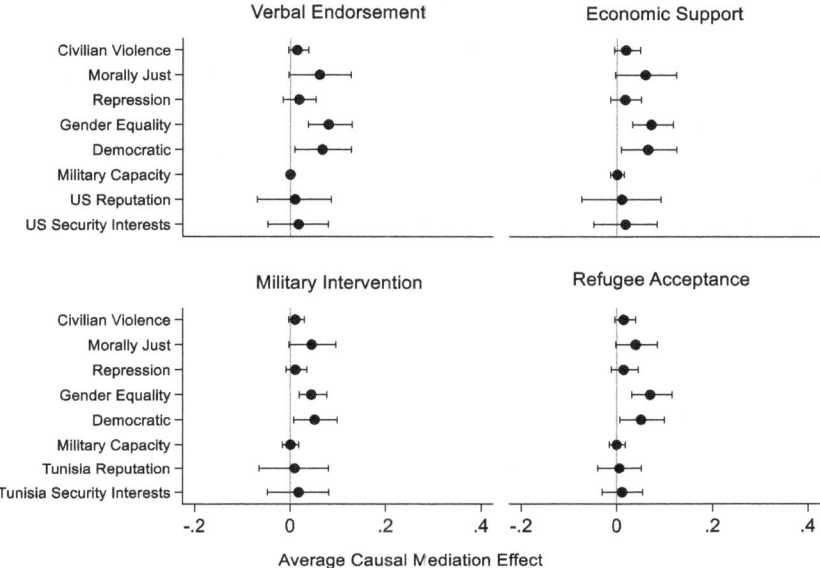

Figure 11 Causal mediation analysis: Tunisia.

Note: The figure represents the effect of the treatment on support levels mediated through each mechanism in the Tunisian sample. Mediation analysis was conducted individually on each mediator using Hicks and Tingley (2011). Lines represent 95 percent confidence intervals. Models are estimated by OLS regression.

rebels' military capacity, or concerns for sponsors' reputation or security interests, are not statistically significant mediators in the US sample.

The results from the Tunisian sample closely mirror those of the US sample (Figure 11). Tunisians who believe that groups with female combatants are more gender equal and democratic are more likely to favor getting involved in the conflict and supporting the insurgency. The effect of female combatants, mediated through perceptions of the insurgency's gender equality and democracy, increases support by approximately 0.07 and 0.06, respectively ($p < 0.05$). Notably, this effect is statistically significant across all support categories, including military intervention, which received low support initially in the absence of the mediated effect of the gender-equal and democratic perception of gender-diverse groups. This means that, while the presence of female combatants alone does not directly lead to favoring military intervention, perceiving them as proponents of democracy and egalitarian values does. Tunisians' support for gender-diverse armed groups is also influenced by the perception that these groups are fighting a morally just war, a factor that does not apply to male combatants. When seen as fighting for a moral cause, female combatants increase support for the Tunisian government's verbal endorsement, economic assistance, military intervention, and accepting refugees by around 0.05 ($p < 0.1$), highlighting the mediating role of moral justification in shaping support for gender-diverse armed groups in Tunisia. That said, the effect sizes in the Tunisian sample are lower than in the US sample (approximately 75 percent for perceived gender equality and 50 percent for perceived democracy).

Other hypothesized mechanisms, such as the strength of the insurgency, government repression, or considerations about the reputation or interests of the sponsoring state, do not seem to mediate the supporting gender-diverse rebel groups; when these perceptions are mediators, the mediated treatment effect is very small, and statistically insignificant in both samples.

The findings are important as they indicate that Tunisians place a high value on gender equality and democracy, to the extent that they are willing to support military intervention on behalf of armed groups that include female combatants. They again challenge the assumption that women stepping out of traditional roles would deter more conservative audiences from offering support. On the contrary, the inclusion of women in combat roles can enhance perceptions of an insurgency's legitimacy and moral standing, even in more traditional societies.

I further explore whether there is a variation in how male versus female respondents evaluate rebel groups in the US and Tunisian samples (Figures A2.5.1 and A2.5.2 in the Appendix). The mediated effects of the treatment on support levels, run separately for male and female respondents, show that men's and women's responses are broadly similar. However, American women's support for insurgencies with female fighters is more strongly influenced by perceptions that the group's tactics are morally justified, and that it is democratic and gender-equal; these factors have about twice and one-and-a-half times more influence on women's support than American men's. In contrast, gender differences are less pronounced among Tunisians. Both Tunisian men and women value the group's perceived gender equality about the same when deciding their level of support. However, Tunisian women are more responsive to the belief that groups with female fighters face greater repression, which increases their support, compared to Tunisian men. Apart from these minor differences, the mechanisms driving support for rebel groups are largely consistent across genders in both samples.

In sum, evidence from survey experiments shows that foreign publics are more likely to favor supporting rebel groups when female fighters are visibly present. American citizens, in particular, are more likely to support their government's decision to verbally endorse, send economic aid to, and accept refugees from the conflict region if the organization includes women militants.

This support is largely driven by the perception that the rebel group is more democratic and gender-egalitarian for both Americans and Tunisians. The findings further suggest that, contrary to the assumption in gender in conflict research, people do not think that the repression by the adversary must be severe if women are fighting. Also, there is no evidence that the presence of women signals the weakness of the armed group. Instead, groups with women militants are perceived to use less violence against civilians (especially in the Tunisian sample) and to engage more in moral conduct (particularly in the US sample). The findings align with the research underlining the importance of normative and humanitarian reasons driving support for the use of force abroad (Kreps and Maxey, 2018), as opposed to the instrumental gains for the sponsoring state.

While overall support for gender-diverse groups is similar between male and female respondents in both samples, American women show a greater increase in support for the insurgency when they see women involved compared to American men. Similarly, Tunisian women demonstrate a larger rise in support for verbal endorsement than Tunisian men when female combatants are present. These results are important because they prompt a reconsideration of the women–peace hypothesis, which suggests a positive linear link between being women and violence-averse attitudes. Studies suggest that women are less likely to support war or the use of force abroad compared to men; however, they have not tested how women react to conflict when women are the perpetrators of violence (Eichenberg, 2003; Wood and Ramirez, 2018). In this Element, while women generally show lower baseline levels of support for conflict abroad than men, their support increases more than men's when they see women insurgents involved in the conflict.

Additionally, the results are largely consistent across both Tunisian and American citizens, defying the expectations of a backlash against female combatants in more conservative societies. In effect, Tunisians with stronger gender-unequal attitudes show higher support for groups with female combatants, indicating that female combatants may enhance the perceived legitimacy of the conflict even more so for more conservative audiences.

These findings suggest that higher support for gender-diverse insurgencies is deeply rooted in gender stereotypes that persist even when confronted with contradictory information that women are perpetrators of violence. Rather than acknowledging women's capacity for violence, respondents maintain the belief that women are inherently peaceful: They view groups with female combatants as less violent, more morally just, and aligned with inclusive ideologies.[11] This tendency to cling to preexisting gendered expectations, even when faced with disconfirming evidence, highlights how deeply entrenched these societal beliefs about women's peacefulness are.

Finally, the treatment design strictly isolates female combatants' distinct impact on support, stripping away the common positive frames of media portraying them as gender-equality or peace activists, mothers, or physically attractive, discussed extensively in Sections 2 and 3. Male combatants, on the other hand, are typically depicted through technical issues regarding combat effectiveness and conflict dynamics. The survey experiments show that, even in the absence of rebel propaganda or media framing, audiences project their own beliefs onto female rebels and perceive them positively compared to males. This suggests that in real-world settings, female combatants may have an even greater influence on public opinion.

4 Foreign Power Support and Gender-Diverse Insurgencies: Observational Analysis

"Amal embraced the ideals of a democratic nation and joined the ranks. She became a fighter for women's liberation."[12] This statement about a female fighter from the SDF website, written in English for foreign audiences, illustrates how rebels frame women's conflict participation as rooted in democratic values and gender equality, mirroring the public perceptions found in the experimental analysis. The survey experiments in the US and Tunisia demonstrate that the presence of female combatants in armed groups increases foreign support for sponsoring these groups. Normative concerns drive this support: Groups with gender-diverse cadres are perceived to be more egalitarian, more democratic, and less violent.

If the results of the survey experiment hold for democracies more broadly, I expect democracies to be more likely to support rebel groups with female combatants compared to those that exclude female combatants, *all else being equal*. There are two main reasons why women's presence might matter for decision-makers: They can help justify foreign involvement to domestic audiences and signal shared liberal values to the decision-makers themselves, which can shape leaders' support for rebel groups.

First, experimental results suggest that supporting groups with female combatants would be more easily justifiable to domestic audiences. Backing organizations with female fighters would be less likely to be considered an act of

---

[11] While female combatants are generally seen as less violent and more morally just in both groups, the reduction in perceived violence is statistically significant among Americans, and the increase in moral legitimacy is significant among Tunisians.

[12] SDF, June 24,2024. https://sdf-press.com/en/?p=17731.

adventurism by the constituents and less likely to create a public uproar. The presence of women would give a positive moral spin to governments' decision to get involved in a foreign conflict. Leaders can anticipate that they can market the decision to support a group of female fighters more easily to the public. I expect this effect to be salient in democracies, where leaders are more responsive to public preferences because the political system holds leaders accountable. Supporting groups lacking public approval could be politically damaging, allowing the opposition to undermine the ruling party, and could be costly for a state's domestic and international reputation (Salehyan, Siroky, and Wood, 2014).

The second reason democracies may favor groups with female members is their signaling of shared liberal values, which is crucial in addressing information asymmetry between principals (states) and agents (rebel groups). States have incomplete information about the interests or ideologies of rebel groups (Salehyan, 2010). Without accurate information beforehand, states risk choosing unreliable or ill-suited agents. To reduce this risk, states look for signs of alignment between their interests and those of the rebels. Ethnic, religious, or linguistic ties are often seen as indicators of shared goals (Salehyan, 2010). The presence of female fighters can similarly become a signal of shared liberal values, like democracy and gender equality, for democracies, as evidenced in the experimental analysis. This perspective can extend beyond the public to decision-makers because they are often tasked with making strategic decisions under uncertainty. They may rely on the symbolic value of female participation in rebel groups as a proxy for broader liberal ideals.

4.1 Public Opinion, Foreign Policy, and Conflict Support

Does public opinion shape foreign policy decisions on external conflict support, and to what extent? First, *the public* involves many non-state actors: Not only the general citizens but also foreign policy professionals, think-tank experts, academics, business leaders, the media, international organization staff, religious leaders, government officials, military personnel, lobbyists, diaspora communities, and activists can influence the decision-making calculus of leaders. These include, for example, the leadership of the International Committee of the Red Cross (ICRC), which urged the Irish Free State's Foreign Minister to follow the Geneva Conventions in 1923 (Sivakumaran, 2012), or the Israeli lobby, which plays a decisive role in US foreign policy, or diasporas such as Norway's Somali community, which directed the Norwegian response to Ethiopia's intervention in Somalia, with then-Secretary of State Johansen stating, "It is important to have a dialogue with the diaspora [since] Somali voters can determine who gets power in Oslo" (Tellander and Horst, 2019: 144).

Does public opinion impact elite foreign policy decisions? Literature argues that audience attitudes influence state behavior by shaping leaders' incentives and constraints (Holsti, 1992; Schultz, 2001; Tomz, 2007). Responsiveness to public opinion and the risk of domestic backlash for unfulfilled commitments – known as audience costs – underpin democratic accountability and democratic peace theory (Fearon, 1994; Tomz and Weeks, 2013; Tomz, Weeks, and Yarhi-Milo, 2020). While post-WWII scholars viewed public opinion as incoherent and irrelevant, recent studies with sophisticated methods suggest a consensus that public opinion shapes leaders' choices (Kertzer and Zeitzoff, 2017). Examples abound: Waning support for the Vietnam War constrained further US interventions (Holsti, 1992). Canadian opposition to the Iraq War prevented troop deployment, despite elite preferences (Goldsmith and Horiuchi, 2012). Intense public backlash after American casualties in Somalia led to the US withdrawal in 1993 (Logan, 1996).

Recent research provides direct evidence, by conducting survey experiments with elites, that policymakers adjust their choices in response to public preferences. Israeli parliament members are more likely to support military strikes in Lebanon when public approval is high and believe that the disapproval of the public would entail heavy political costs (Tomz et al., 2020). Members of the UK's House of Commons favor military patrols in the South China Sea more when the public shows greater support (Chu and Recchia, 2022). When the public favors increasing sanctions against Russia, US foreign policy practitioners are more likely to support stronger sanctions (Peez and Bethke, 2025). Even non-elected US military officers are more willing to engage in operations in Somalia when the public endorses intervention (Lin-Greenberg, 2021).

A large body of work argues that public sentiment matters for foreign decisions, not only in democracies but in hybrid and authoritarian states, as their survival is also dependent on legitimacy in the eyes of the people (Li and Chen, 2021; Weeks, 2008; Weiss, 2014; Weis and Dafoe, 2019). China's "Wolf Warrior" diplomacy reflects the government's need to appease nationalist audiences, despite international ineffectiveness (Mattingly and Sundquist, 2023). As the US pushed for allies in the Iraq invasion, Turkey's parliament blocked US access due to overwhelming public opposition, despite the initial Erdoğan–Bush agreement, as the parliament "ultimately chose to listen to the voice of the public opinion, not to that of the government leadership" (Goldsmith and Horiuchi, 2012: 567). In the 1960s, Tunisian President Bourguiba's pragmatic stance toward Israel clashed with domestic sentiment, sparking mass protests during the 1967 Six-Day War, forcing him to avoid full normalization with Israel (Ghiles-Meilhac, 2014). Pro-Iraq demonstrations in Tunisia during the Second Gulf War "had a considerable impact on the government's crisis behavior, dissuading the government from associating with Israel" (Abadi, 2017: 519).

That said, audience costs in authoritarian regimes depend on certain conditions, such as regime type (personalist vs. single-party regimes), elite dynamics (military-backed leaders facing greater costs), and media control (Slantchev, 2006; Svolik, 2012; Weeks, 2012). These suggest that while autocracies face some constraints, democratic leaders are more accountable to the public, the opposition, and civil society. Therefore, I focus on democracies, where public influence on leaders' decisions is strongest.

With ample evidence of domestic actors' influence on international affairs, the debate has shifted from whether it matters to how it shapes decisions and which arguments sway publics and elites. Elite factions try to establish a dominant narrative because broadening coalitions legitimizes conflict intervention and minimizes political costs. Given the high costs, reducing internal repercussions of conflict engagement abroad is deemed to be central to foreign policy decision-making (Krebs and Jackson, 2007). Maxey (2020) finds that humanitarian claims, sometimes more effective than security-based arguments, maximize domestic support for sponsorship decisions. Even in polarized contexts, framing interventions as humanitarian increases public approval (Hildebrandt et al., 2013). Consequently, both rebel groups and foreign governments use humanitarian narratives through public diplomacy to restore legitimacy and preempt elite opposition, to reach not only policymakers but also the broader public through meetings, media campaigns, and opinion pieces (Mattiacci and Jones, 2020).

For instance, Kuwait hired the US PR firm Hill & Knowlton to secure US support against Iraq's invasion, framing Kuwait as a progressive ally by highlighting women's ability to drive in Kuwait. Surveys showed that this gendered narrative resonated with US audiences, mobilizing support (Mattiacci and Jones, 2020). Nepal's Maoists successfully lobbied with India by framing their government as repressive, and held mass solidarity rallies in Delhi to pressure the Nepali government (Mishra, 2024). The Maoists' inclusive approach toward female militants further bolstered their legitimacy (Giri, 2023) (see also the SDF example at the beginning of Section 1). These examples show that rebels recognize the value of cultivating public support to catalyze foreign governments' conflict assistance.

This does not mean that the presence of female fighters determines the direction of all foreign support, nor do I suggest that it is the sole or primary factor influencing the decision to provide support. States may sponsor rebel groups for a variety of reasons, with the main motive being the rebels' ability to advance the sponsoring government's objectives. However, sponsors can be driven by various ideological or domestic motivations (Gelpi et al., 2009; San-Akca, 2016), and public attitudes create incentives for conflict involvement, as political costs arise when governments go against these preferences (Tomz and Weeks, 2013).

To understand if the survey results reflect a larger trend and have practical consequences in foreign policy decisions to sponsor armed organizations, I analyze whether gender-diverse groups are more likely to attract support from democracies. Given that the public cares about the decency of governments' actions (Kertzer et al., 2014), and policymakers are responsive to the public in democracies, I expect rebel groups with female fighters to be more likely to be supported by democracies.

H1: Rebel groups with female combatants are more likely to receive support from democracies than those without female combatants.

4.2 Data and Research Design

To test the hypothesis, I use the expanded Non-State Actors in Conflict (NSA) dataset by Cunningham, Gleditsch, and Salehyan (2009), which provides information on external state supporters of rebel groups. The NSA dataset covers 1989 to 2009 and contains all the conflict cases in the UCDP (Uppsala Conflict Data Program) Dyadic Dataset (Harbom, Melander, and Wallensteen, 2008). The unit of analysis is the rebel organization–adversary state dyad. The support can be in the form of endorsement, non-military (i.e., economic) assistance, military assistance (i.e., weapons, equipment, training), or sending troops on the ground.[13]

I capture whether rebels receive support from democratic countries using two measures. The first is *democratic support*, which identifies the regime type of foreign sponsors. This binary measure captures whether an armed organization ever received support from a democracy in its lifespan. This is operationalized by matching the foreign powers with their Polity scores, with states scoring 6 or higher on the combined Polity IV scale classified as democratic sponsors (Marshall, Gurr, and Jaggers, 2017). To assess if female combatants attract a greater concentration of democratic sponsors, I employ

---

[13] The analysis does not distinguish between these types because the small number of observations for each support type does not allow for reliable statistical inference. Also, groups often receive a combination of support types, making differentiating them difficult. Scholars also argue that publicly endorsing rebels' objectives as "just" can sometimes be just as important a form of support as more direct aid, such as providing arms (San-Akca, 2016).

a second measure, *democratic proportion*, operationalized as the proportion of democratic supporters to all foreign supporters. This follows the operationalization of Salehyan et al. (2014), who examined the relationship between democratic sponsorship and rebel-inflicted civilian violence.

This measure does not distinguish between overt and covert support; hence, it captures both. This aligns with the theoretical argument. If democratic publics view the group more favorably due to female fighters' perceived gender equality and democracy, overt support is more likely. However, if female combatants serve as a signal to leaders among other rebels in an environment of information asymmetry – operating through elite perception rather than public opinion – then covert support is also plausible. Since both support types are consistent with the argument, and given the unreliability of covert support data, I do not distinguish between them in the analysis.

To operationalize the independent variable, the presence of *female combatants*, I use the Women in Armed Rebellion Dataset (WARD) (Wood and Thomas, 2017), which covers information on female fighters' presence for a cross-national sample of rebel organizations based on the UCDP Dyadic Dataset (Harbom et al., 2008). Based on the UN definition, WARD defines female fighters as combatants "employed in frontline combat, female suicide bombers or assassins, and female auxiliaries or members of civil defense forces who receive military training, carry combat weapons, and could be called upon to participate in combat when necessary" (Wood and Thomas, 2017: 38). It captures whether a rebel organization recruits female fighters or not. This binary measure ensures focus on their presence, capturing whether women are involved in combat irrespective of their prevalence, which rebel groups often exaggerate to gain international attention (see Section 2.1). I include a second independent variable – female combatant prevalence – to measure whether the proportion of women matters for foreign support. This ordinal variable ranges from 0 to 3 (0 indicates no evidence of female fighters, 1 for less than 5 percent, 2 for 5–20 percent, and 3 for more than 20 percent women in the group from WARD). These measures exclude female members in noncombat positions, such as cooks, nurses, and couriers, which aligns with this Element's theoretical focus on attitudes toward women who disrupt traditional gender norms. Female fighters attract more visibility and attention because they challenge these norms, while women in support roles are viewed as more typical.

I account for potential confounding factors as various conflict dynamics and rebel group characteristics can influence both state support for foreign armed groups and female recruitment. States are generally reluctant to engage in prolonged conflicts or those with high casualties due to concerns about managing their complexities (Aydin, 2010; Balch-Lindsay, Enterline, and Joyce,

2008; Regan, 2002). These also impact female recruitment; rebels engaged in longer-lasting (Wood and Allemang, 2022) and high-casualty conflicts are more likely to recruit women to replenish their ranks (Thomas and Bond, 2015). I account for *conflict duration*, defined as the number of years since the conflict's onset, and *conflict intensity*, measured by the number of battle-related deaths according to the UCDP Battle-Related Deaths Dataset (Allansson, Melander, and Themnér, 2017).

Shifting the focus to rebel group characteristics, stronger groups can be better positioned for external support as they can challenge the target government effectively and ensure security for female participants (Salehyan et al., 2011; Thomas and Bond, 2015). *Troop size* is measured using the best estimate of average rebel troop size from the NSA dataset. To account for rebel capabilities relative to the state, following Manekin and Wood (2020), I control for *very weak rebels*, indicating whether the aggregate military capabilities of the organization were "much weaker" than those of the state, from the NSA dataset (both rescaled by dividing by 1,000). Additionally, competition among rebel organizations can influence both external support and the inclusion of female fighters in recruitment strategies. As competition intensifies, groups are pressured to distinguish themselves, modify their ideologies (Tokdemir et al., 2020), cater more to sponsor demands, and address the heightened demand for fighters (Bob, 2005; Walter, 2015). *Rebel competition* is quantified by the number of groups fighting within the same conflict. Also, armed groups with transnational diasporas can better secure external support, as these communities can lobby their governments on their behalf (Salehyan et al., 2011). The mean of the *transnational constituencies' support* is adopted from the NSA dataset. Further, groups that coerce civilians, including women, may project an image of radical violence rather than inclusivity. The hypothesized relationship linking female combatants to increased support may not work if the groups recruit women by force, as they would not be associated with desirable ideologies like democracy or gender equality (Braithwaite and Ruiz, 2018). This aspect is captured using a binary measure of *forced recruitment* from Cohen (2013), reflecting the use of abduction, press-ganging, or other coercive recruitment strategies.

Finally, I control for two state-level characteristics. I account for the strategic importance of the civil war-experiencing country using the Composite Index of National Capability (CINC) score (Singer, 1988). Stronger states can discourage others from funding their insurgents' activities, or rebels operating against stronger states may be viewed as less likely to be successful (Salehyan et al., 2011). *Target state power* controls for this deterrent effect of being a powerful country, which I log to manage outliers. *Target state regime type* is another state-level variable controlling for the Polity score of the adversary state against which the rebels are fighting. Respecting the legitimacy of a democratically elected government has become a rather salient norm in the post–Cold War era, especially for democratic states. Alternatively, operating in a democratic country may affect the rebel group's ability to establish connections with external actors (Manekin and Wood, 2020).

4.3 Analysis

I calculate the models using OLS regression, which is more robust for modeling misspecification and distribution assumptions (Angrist and Pischke, 2008). The observational data used here is time-invariant because WARD is time-invariant; hence, there is a single observation per rebel group.

This can affect the interpretation of the relationship and warrants a note on endogeneity. My theory suggests that rebel groups with female combatants are more likely to receive support from democratic states, which view their inclusion as rendering the group a less adventurous and more legitimate endeavor, largely because public opinion favors women fighters. This awareness could drive democratic sponsors to influence rebel group composition strategically, having the rebel groups recruit women or at least advertise women *after* they support the insurgency. This dynamic is consistent with my argument because it indicates that leaders are aware of the legitimization that women bring to armed groups. Conversely, rebel groups recognizing the value of such support may strategically adjust their composition to include female combatants in response to this demand. This again aligns with the essence of my theory, and I expect both processes to be at work. Also, whether rebels strategically manipulate democratic values to gain support or genuinely adapt to them is an intriguing question with implications for stability and credibility, though this lies beyond the scope of this Element. Ultimately, whether democracies support female fighters to cater to public opinion, or rebel groups adjust their composition in response, or sponsors promote female inclusion, all pathways highlight the correlation between democratic sponsors and female combatants as indicators of legitimacy and commitment to democratic ideals within armed groups.

Another consideration is the possibility of spurious correlation: Do rebel groups with female fighters engage in causes that democracies already support? Is it the nature of the cause, rather than the presence of women, that attracts democratic backing? The analysis here does not directly test this possibility. However, historical trends suggest that female participation has been more common among Marxist-oriented leftist groups (Wood and Thomas, 2017), where gender equality is often central to their ideology. But during the Cold

War, Western democracies actively opposed communist movements and backed their adversaries. The US, the most active supporter of rebel groups, primarily funded anti-Marxist forces. This suggests that the causes that groups with female militants fight for have not inherently aligned with causes backed by democracies, which can mitigate concerns about spurious correlation.

The results support the hypothesis. The presence of female combatants is positively associated with both the likelihood of receiving support from democratic states and the proportion of democratic supporters. According to Model 1 in Table 2, rebel groups with female combatants are 19 percent more likely to gain democratic support ($p < 0.05$). In Model 2, groups with female combatants have an 18 percent higher proportion of democratic supporters ($p < 0.05$). Model 3 shows that each one-unit increase in the female prevalence category (i.e., moving from 0 to 1, or from 1 to 2) is associated with an 11 percentage point increase in the probability that a rebel group receives support from a democratic sponsor. Model 4 suggests that a higher proportion of female combatants is correlated with attracting a higher proportion of democratic supporters. These findings show that when rebel groups include female combatants, democratic states are more likely to support them, compared to groups without female combatants. This aligns with the experimental evidence suggesting that female combatants signal a form of inclusivity in a way that attracts support from democratic regimes.

I check for the robustness of the models in several ways (see the Appendix). First, I estimate the same models via probit and ordered probit, respectively, instead of OLS (Models 1 and 2, Table A12). Second, I estimate models accounting for rebel group ideology, particularly *leftist* and *Islamist* ideologies (Models 3 and 4, Table A12), as these can influence the presence of female fighters and the likelihood of foreign support (Wood and Thomas, 2017). Leftist groups, which tend to recruit more women, at the same time may alienate foreign powers opposed to their revolutionary agendas. In contrast, Islamist groups are less likely to recruit women, and may influence foreign perceptions negatively, as media portrayals in the West are highly racialized, and female militants in rebel groups pertaining to radical extremist interpretations of Islam are often vilified, ridiculed, or shown as the embodiment of the epitome of jihadist evil, as seen in the coverage of ISIS (Kollárová, 2015). These portrayals may diminish the chances of favorable foreign support.

Thid, I estimate the models excluding transnational support and very weak rebels (Models 5 and 6, Table A12). I expect transnational support to operate through similar hypothesized mechanisms; transnational constituencies, such as

Table 2 Female combatants and democratic support

	Model 1 Democratic support	Model 2 Proportion of democratic support	Model 3 Democratic support	Model 4 Proportion of democratic support
Female combatants	0.193**	0.181**		
	(0.094)	(0.075)		
Female combatants prevalence			0.111**	0.112***
			(0.050)	(0.040)
Duration	0.018**	0.008	0.016*	0.006
	(0.008)	(0.005)	(0.008)	(0.006)
Conflict intensity	−0.011	−0.012	−0.019	−0.020*
	(0.019)	(0.009)	(0.019)	(0.011)
Rebel troop size	0.004***	0.001	0.004***	0.001
	(0.001)	(0.001)	(0.001)	(0.001)
Very weak rebels	−0.003	−0.014	0.007	−0.004
	(0.089)	(0.079)	(0.085)	(0.075)
Rebel competition	0.002	0.001	0.002	0.002
	(0.008)	(0.006)	(0.008)	(0.006)
Forced recruitment	−0.106	−0.089	−0.104	−0.090
	(0.097)	(0.070)	(0.096)	(0.069)
Transconstitutional support	0.034	0.016	0.051	0.032
	(0.047)	(0.040)	(0.047)	(0.038)
Target state regime	−0.016**	−0.011*	−0.017**	−0.012**
	(0.008)	(0.006)	(0.008)	(0.006)
Target state power	0.085***	0.076***	0.086***	0.077***
	(0.030)	(0.027)	(0.029)	(0.027)
Constant	0.569**	0.536**	0.580**	0.548**
	(0.240)	(0.214)	(0.233)	(0.207)
Observations	120	120	119	119
R-squared	0.327	0.268	0.329	0.283

Note: Robust standard errors clustered by conflict in parentheses ***$p<0.01$, ** $p<0.05$, * $p<0.1$.

diaspora communities or INGOs, may also be influenced by gender stereotypes that attach humanitarian or normatively desirable values to female fighters. I also estimate models excluding very weak rebel groups to avoid potential collinearity.

The positive and significant relationship between female combatants and democratic support remains consistent across these model specifications, attesting to the robustness of these findings. The results provide a plausibility probe that favorable foreign public opinions toward female combatants can influence democratic leaders' decisions to support gender-diverse groups. The observational data limits my ability to establish causality, hence the results are correlational rather than causal. Nevertheless, they align with the experimental results and confirm hypothesized expectations.

4.4 Discussion

Using survey experiments, I provide causal evidence that the visible presence of female combatants shapes perceptions of rebel groups as embodying gender equality, democracy, moral legitimacy, and reduced civilian violence, which enhances foreign support for these groups. Observational analysis further indicates that groups with female combatants are more likely to receive backing from democratic states, suggesting that favorable perceptions can translate into concrete advantages. These results raise two important questions: First, is there an objective difference between groups with and without female combatants regarding their adherence to morally desirable wartime strategies? Second, if women's presence can benefit rebel groups, why do not all groups recruit women, or at least market themselves as having them?

4.4.1 Do Groups with Female Combatants Actually Adhere More to Moral Wartime Strategies?

The first question's analysis is beyond this Element's scope, but existing literature offers insights. Research challenges the perception that groups with female combatants use less violence or conduct more ethical wartime behavior. Groups with higher proportions of frontline female fighters tend to engage in increased civilian violence (Harrell, 2023) and are more likely to conduct terrorist attacks (Thomas and Wood, 2018). Furthermore, female suicide bombers often execute more lethal attacks by exploiting the "peaceful woman" stereotype to evade security (Alakoc, 2020; O'Rourke, 2009; Thomas, 2021).

Regarding sexual violence, a key indicator of extremist violence and ethical conduct in conflicts, Cohen (2013) refutes assumptions of female nonviolence by documenting women's regular involvement in sexual violence during the Sierra Leone Civil War. Similar findings from other conflict zones like the Democratic Republic of Congo, Uganda, Rwanda, and Liberia reveal that women's participation in severe human rights violations, including sexual violence, is not an anomaly but is often overlooked as males are presumed to be sole perpetrators and the gender of perpetrators is seldom recorded in national surveys (Cohen, 2013). While these are drawn from single cases, cross-national analyses show mixed evidence on whether female combatants' presence increases or decreases the overall sexual violence conducted by their groups (Loken, 2017; Mehrl, 2022).

Moreover, psychological studies indicate that female combatants exhibit appetitive aggression – positive emotional associations with violent acts – at levels similar to male combatants, reflecting a shared potential to perceive perpetrated violence as fascinating and exciting (Meyer-Parlapanis et al., 2016). No evidence indicates higher levels of regret among women for engaging in undesirable acts of violence, as documented in studies of ex-combatants in Burundi and Colombia (Meyer-Parlapanis et al., 2016; Weierstall et al., 2013).

Gendered dynamics within rebel groups also factor in women's violent acts. Female fighters sometimes resort to more extreme acts of violence to gain acceptance and recognition among male peers who often marginalize women as unfit for combat. For example, the LTTE's female fighters developed a reputation for extreme aggression, which not only instilled fear in opponents but also helped secure their standing and protection among male counterparts (Alison, 2004). Overall, the literature provides no conclusive evidence that rebel groups with female fighters engage in less violence or adopt more normatively desirable behaviors than all-male groups. If anything, their presence may intensify conflict dynamics.

4.4.2 If Female Fighters Offer Such Outreach Benefits, Why Don't All Rebels Recruit Them?

The second question the findings prompt is, if women's presence provides such strategic advantages to rebel groups, why don't all groups recruit or market themselves as having female fighters? While recruiting women can offer several benefits for armed groups, there can also be drawbacks. There are six main negative aspects: disrupting internal cohesion due to male members' refusal of female combatants, difficulty of managing sexual relationships, organizational capacity, concerns for authenticity, repelling support from domestic traditional audiences, and ideological fit.

The first challenge of incorporating women in combat units is regulating inter-member relations. The challenge of coping with male members' refusal to accept women's combat roles can cause incohesion within the units and constrain rebel capabilities (Thomas and Bond, 2015). Rebel groups remain deeply patriarchal, and women's active participation in the traditionally male domain of combat typically creates distress for male members. Male members' distress at fighting side by side with female members has caused inefficiencies even for leftist groups with a high proportion of female fighters that embrace gender-inclusive ideology (Başer, 2022). For instance, female combatants of PKK have been expelled from key units and forced to engage in propaganda activities instead of frontline combat positions due to male members' resentment (PKK, 1999).

The second reason why rebel leaders may hesitate to recruit women is the complexity of managing romantic relationships within the group. Such relationships risk diverting commitment from the cause to a partner, threaten group cohesion by fostering competing loyalties, and increase defections among members, thereby reducing manpower and organizational capacity (Matfess, 2024). Although some leaders address this by tying members' marriage to the rebellion itself, to reinforce the commitment to rebel goals, these romantic relationships impose logistical demands around family and reproductive issues that could detract from military efforts, because managing marital relationships within the group requires careful logistical planning that may exceed the rebels' wartime capabilities (Matfess, 2024). For instance, the forced contraception and abortion policy of Colombia's FARC has strained internal morale and sparked a public backlash (Svallfors, 2024).

Relatedly, the third reason is about organizational capacity and resource constraints. Recruiting, training, and integrating female militants into the group requires organizational capacity and substantial effort, which many groups may lack. For instance, Boko Haram has not provided the required training to the girls and women they forcefully recruited and thus has failed to acquire their tactical advantage (Ryckman and Henshaw, 2025). Similarly, many groups pursuing active fighting can be more focused on combat effectiveness on the ground and survival, rather than investing in integrating women for outreach. If the groups lack the ability to attract or keep women fighters, they may not be positioned to benefit from their tactical advantage.

A fourth reason rebel groups may hesitate to recruit women is the risk of alienating conservative public support, particularly among domestic audiences who disapprove of women abandoning traditional private roles (O'Rourke, 2009). While this Element finds that female combatants can increase support among traditionalist Tunisians, domestic constituencies' opinions may differ depending on the ideology and aim of the rebel groups, and groups modify their behavior to avoid public reaction. Nonreligious rebel groups are more likely to include women as combatants and leaders, while religious groups – sensitive to conservative views – tend to avoid recruiting women to prevent backlash (Loken and Matfess, 2024). Also, rebel leaders may overestimate backlash risks.

That said, conservative organizations sometimes recruit women as well, often later in conflicts as personnel needs become urgent, like the Lord's Resistance Army (LRA), which began recruiting girls only after Ugandan counterinsurgency operations intensified. Even in these cases, conservative groups emphasize traditional gender norms to preserve support, framing women's roles in terms of sacrifice for their children or promising a return to traditional roles post-conflict (Loken, 2021). To further manage perceptions, rebel groups may adjust the visibility and framing of female members, inflating or downplaying their roles strategically to signal alignment with conservative audiences (Szekely, 2020).

Fifth, conservative rebel groups that aim to establish systems restricting women's public roles may view female recruitment as fundamentally incompatible with their political objectives and exclude them based on ideological grounds. An example is the Taliban – now governing Afghanistan.

Finally, if groups just add female militants for the sake of appearances, it could backfire as the supporters – whether local or foreign – might view this as inauthentic or manipulative. Many groups are invested in the narratives and identities that they cultivate. Adding women just for the optics could undermine the group's credibility since external actors might see through the "PR move" and dismiss it as a shallow attempt to gain support.

5 Conclusion

Most rebel groups receive external assistance, which critically impacts conflict dynamics and shifts the balance of power between the rebels and the government they are fighting against. Foreign support tends to prolong conflicts, increase civilian violence, foster factionalism within rebel groups, and complicate peace processes due to the involvement of multiple external actors with competing interests (Heger and Salehyan, 2007; Ives, 2021; Regan, 2002). These important consequences necessitate a deeper understanding of the factors influencing this support. In this Element, I examine how women in armed groups affect foreign support. Drawing from diverse theoretical and empirical literatures in conflict studies, gender, and political psychology, I develop a theoretical framework explaining the unique impact of gendered images of rebel groups in shaping foreign public opinion and elite decision-making strategies, and provide empirical evidence showing that female combatants indeed attract more support from foreign audiences and democratic states.

Scholars have suggested that recruiting women enhances the legitimacy of rebel organizations. However, evidence supporting this claim and the mechanisms through which women increase the organizations' legitimacy has been limited (Manekin and Wood, 2020), and the specific ways gender-diverse organizations are perceived differently have been unexplored. Importantly, we lack understanding of whether promoting female combatants increases public support, and whether this, in turn, leads to tangible state support. Thus, I combined experimental and observational analysis to evaluate female combatants' effects on foreign support for armed groups. This way, I respond to feminist international relations scholars' calls for greater dialogue between gender research and quantitative approaches (Sjoberg, Kadera, and Thies, 2018; Stauffer and O'Brien, 2018).

To begin with, I show that women's involvement in armed groups increases public support for their governments' sponsorship of these groups. I do this via two original survey experiments conducted in different sociocultural regions, with American and Tunisian citizens. This effect is particularly strong in the US, where citizens are more likely to support their government's endorsement – both verbally and financially – and to accept refugees from conflict zones when women are visibly engaged in the conflict.

Further, both Tunisian and American respondents perceive gender-diverse organizations as more gender-equal and democratic. At the same time, the presence of female combatants leads Tunisians to believe that the group uses less violence against civilians, while Americans are more likely to view the group's use of armed struggle as morally justifiable when women are involved. These normative and humanitarian factors are also the key mechanisms that drive public support for gender-diverse organizations.

Contrary to assumptions about societal backlash against women abandoning traditional roles, the data reveal no such response. In fact, traditional gender attitudes unexpectedly increase support for female combatants, particularly among Tunisians. This finding highlights a counterintuitive dynamic: Rather than challenging traditional norms, female fighters may resonate with some conservative audiences, revealing an overlooked impact of gender norms on support for political violence. This is unlikely to be because women gain respect by acting "like men," because experimental findings indicate that audiences continue to project feminine nonviolent virtues onto female fighters. Instead, these individuals may be interpreting women's combatancy through a traditional lens, as women's sacrifice deserving protection. A similar chivalry is displayed by male diplomats in the Council of the European Union, who become more conciliatory toward their female colleagues (Naurin, Naurin, and Alexander, 2019). In contrast, neither those with more progressive gender views, who have already normalized women's public participation, nor conservative Americans show significant change in their support for conflict when women are involved. The difference in support for female combatants among

Tunisian and American conservatives likely stems from domestic norms about women in the military. In the US, where the focus is on women's empowerment and breaking into male-dominated spaces, conservatives may view female fighters as challenging their militarized masculinities. In contrast, in Tunisia, where women's inclusion in the military is often tied to national modernization reforms, conservatives, perhaps socialized in honor culture, view female fighters through a protective lens, rather than as a challenge to gender norms. The data does not directly test these interpretations, offering a useful avenue for further research.

Another important finding relates to gendered preferences on the use of force. Extant literature suggests that women are less likely to support the use of violence in foreign policy decisions. Yet, women's attitudes toward the use of force are typically tested in scenarios where the perpetrators are men, rather than women. This Element shows that the gender gap in support for political violence narrows when women are the perpetrators. While the increase in support for female combatants does not differ significantly between male and female respondents, female respondents also demonstrate a significant rise in support – even slightly higher – when they see female combatants compared to male combatants. This finding suggests a reconsideration of the gender gap in support of the use of force documented in the literature, as it reveals that female respondents show increased support when combatants are women. Mediation analyses further suggest that women's increased support is primarily driven by the perception associating female combatants with the fight for gender equality; the presence of female combatants increases perceptions of group commitment to gender equality, which in turn boosts support for the group. This shift indicates that women relate differently to conflict scenarios involving female fighters, potentially viewing them through lenses of empowerment and solidarity, which challenges typical assumptions about gendered attitudes toward violence. This conclusion is essential for the "women/gender equality and peace hypothesis," discussed further later.

Additionally, using observational data on foreign states' support for armed groups, I examine the tangible impact that female combatants can have on conflict dynamics. The presence of female fighters increases the likelihood of democratic states supporting these groups. This suggests that favorable public opinion toward female combatants may shape foreign leaders' decisions in democracies, where leaders are more responsive to public sentiment. Additionally, female combatants may act as a heuristic for shared liberal values, such as democracy and gender equality, which could also motivate democratic leaders to back these groups. Thus, female participation in armed groups provides foreign leaders an opportunity to align their decisions with public opinion or to interpret the presence of women as an indicator of compatible ideological values.

The results of this Element are important, first and foremost, because they reveal how female combatants uniquely influence conflict dynamics, enabling rebel groups to secure external support and attract allies, thereby impacting their survival and success. Existing research on external support in civil wars generally assumes that foreign governments base decisions on strategic calculations, overlooking how rebels craft narratives and ensure visibility to gain support (Huang, 2016). I demonstrate that the gendered imagery of rebel organizations shapes outreach strategies, audience perceptions, and international support. This way, this Element contributes to literatures on third-party involvement in civil wars, rebel reputation, and marketing by highlighting gender composition as a significant factor in these areas. Also, showing that female combatants attract more foreign support due to signaling humanitarian values and ideological moderation, the results expand prior work showing that the public cares about moral concerns in foreign policy decisions and that susceptibility to international audiences can shape rebel behavior (Jo, 2015; Lupu and Wallace, 2024; Stanton, 2016).

Second, I extend work at the intersection of gender, conflict, and international relations showing that war is not gender-neutral: gendered logics shape judgments about war and international politics (Sjoberg, 2013). Specifically, I shift focus from why women join to how their participation reshapes conflict dynamics. While considerable progress has been made in understanding gendered dynamics within conflicts, much existing research remains centered on women's motivations for joining these groups. Expanding this focus allows new avenues to examine the complex relationship among women, gender equality, and political violence. Notably, this emphasis contributes to, and problematizes, the women–peace or "gender equality–peace" hypothesis, which suggests a positive linear relationship among women, gender equality, and peace.

Empirical studies building the foundation of the women–peace hypothesis show that as gender equality increases (e.g., lower fertility rates, more women in the labor market, education, and politics), the likelihood of domestic and international conflict declines, whereas lower levels of gender equality result in higher chances of armed conflict (Caprioli and Boyer, 2001; Demeritt, Nichols, and Kelly, 2014; Hudson et al., 2009; Melander, 2005). These arguments are reflected at the individual level too; studies show that women and those who hold more progressive gender-egalitarian attitudes are less likely to support war, the use of violence, or military intervention (McDermott and Cowden, 2001; Tessler and Warriner, 1997; Wood and Ramirez, 2018).

According to this view, women are often socialized toward nonviolence, expected to embody traditionally feminine traits such as cooperation, compassion, and pacifism. At the same time, how women are treated in society establishes a broader model for how others are treated, where women's systematic domination normalizes violence and coercion as acceptable methods for resolving conflicts. As such, support for political violence should decline within societies that embrace gender equality. Also, within the patriarchal system, war and violence are often seen as masculine traditions, with men feeling pressure to uphold aggressive behaviors to maintain gendered hierarchies (Goldstein, 2001). These norms lead men to support aggression and violence. As men's beliefs about gender equality become more progressive, their support for violence declines (Wood and Ramirez, 2018).

The findings of this Element highlight a more complex relationship between women or gender equality and peace for four reasons. First, I show that women can help sustain violence by attracting foreign support and encouraging third-party involvement. Second, I demonstrate that female militants – the perpetrators of violence – could signal gender equality and make their armed groups look more gender-equal. This differs from the gender equality–peace hypothesis as it suggests that groups using violent tactics, hence perpetuating war, are not viewed in contrast to gender-equal values; on the contrary, they are perceived to embody gender equality. Third, people's willingness to provide more support to groups with female combatants is primarily driven by the thinking that these groups are gender equal, suggesting that gender equality can contribute to the prevalence of violent strategies. This counters the expectation that the spread of gender-equal attitudes might decline support for violence – at least when women are perpetrators. Fourth, while women show lower base levels of getting involved in a conflict abroad than men, their support increases more than men's, albeit slightly, when they see women militants involved in the conflict. This, again, defies the expectations regarding women's lower levels of support for the use of force. Women respond more positively to female combatants perhaps because they identify with them or perceive their participation as a form of empowerment. This response complicates the women–peace hypothesis by indicating that women's opposition to conflict is not absolute but can shift based on gender representation within armed groups. While the results also show that those with gender-equal attitudes overall are less likely to favor supporting insurgencies of any type, more focused analyses highlight the multifaceted nature of the relationship among women, gender equality, and violence. They suggest that arguments concerning the role of gender equality in conflict should take organizational differences and the gender of the perpetrators into account.

The third venue to which my findings contribute is the broader scholarship on the consequences of women's political participation. Research shows that women's representation in decision-making enhances the perceived legitimacy of those procedures – citizens view them as less corrupt, fairer, and more democratic (Barnes and Beaulieu, 2019; Clayton et al., 2019). These studies confirm the expectations of democratic theorists because political offices lack legitimacy when certain groups are systematically excluded (Dovi, 2007). This legitimizing effect is not surprising in democratic settings where women's involvement in decision-making is a fundamental democratic principle. However, this Element demonstrates that women evoke similarly positive perceptions in nontraditional political realms, such as warfare – even as perpetrators of violence and even when rebel groups do not typically uphold or are expected to uphold democratic norms. The presence of female combatants boosts a rebel group's perceived legitimacy and democratic credentials

These findings bridge the gender in conflict with authoritarianism literatures. Research shows that, in autocracies, increased representation of women enhances perceptions of democracy and legitimacy and elevates international aid and reputation for these regimes (Bush and Zetterberg, 2021; Bush et al., 2024). Radical-right parties strategically boost women's representation to soften their extremist image and broaden appeal beyond their base (Ben-Shitrit, Elad-Strenger, and Hirsch-Hoefler, 2022; Weeks et al., 2023). This Element demonstrates that, much like in democracies, autocracies, and radical-right parties, rebel groups can all rely on female representation to shape perceptions of legitimacy and expand support. Highlighting this shared mechanism across diverse political settings connects these separate literatures, showing how gender inclusivity serves as a strategic tool for gaining broader support across state and non-state actors.

Fourth, this Element demonstrates that deeply ingrained beliefs about women as compassionate, peaceful, and passive persist even when confronted with evidence of women's capacity for violence. These existing beliefs or embedded expectations influence interpretations of evidence, leading them to update the armed groups' strategies as less violent and more moral, instead of updating beliefs about women's potential as perpetrators. This aligns with the literature demonstrating that people assimilate data into beliefs rather than adjusting those beliefs in line with the new information (Mercer, 2010). This is also in line with more recent research indicating that exposure to counter-stereotypes fails to alter respondents' generic core beliefs about women and men (Jung and Tavits, 2024). In the case of female combatants, the perception of a rebel group as a cohesive unit allows observers to use gender cues to infer traits like moderation and righteousness. These impressions are reinforced by limited information about rebel groups and media portrayals shaped by gender stereotypes. Projecting entrenched beliefs about "peaceful women" onto violent groups helps reconcile this contradiction. The results are striking because historically communist insurgencies were most active in recruiting female fighters – driven by Marxist, not democratic, ideals within class struggle contexts, which Western democracies actively sought to undermine. Today, female combatants signal democratic principles despite this history. This shift reflects the global spread of Western ideals linking gender equality with democracy, conslidated as Western powers tied foreign aid to promote both democracy and women's rights. As a result, female fighters are now more closely associated with democratic legitimacy despite their historical ties to communism.

Finally, this Element suggests that democratic and gender-equal principles can be leveraged to sustain armed groups' violent strategies and be instrumentalized for political gain. This has policy implications. The observed advantages of recruiting women may incentivize more rebel groups to attract women into their ranks. This strategy can place women in dangerous situations and open up new insecurities, from the risk of being killed by counterinsurgency efforts or by conducting suicide attacks to being marginalized by male combatants within the hypermasculine rebel group settings. Similar incentives may also lead state militaries to increase female representation within their ranks. This has the potential to advance gender equality within the security sector – a desirable outcome. However, there is a risk that it will become merely symbolic, instrumentalizing women for political aims rather than addressing deeper systematic inequalities within these typically patriarchal institutions. Policymakers must understand that gender norms play a critical role in countering drivers of violent radicalization. At the same time, they should also avoid the "add women and stir" approach, as the relationship between gender and violence is more complex.

Appendix

A1 Experimental Outcomes

- **Verbal endorsement:** Please indicate how strongly you agree or disagree with the following statement: The United States/Tunisia should verbally endorse the Moravian insurgent group.
- **Economic support:** Please indicate how strongly you agree or disagree with the following statement: The United States/Tunisia should provide economic support to the Moravian insurgent group.
- **Military intervention:** Please indicate how strongly you agree or disagree with the following statement: The United States/Tunisia should militarily intervene on behalf of the Moravian insurgent group to fight the adversary Falconian state forces.
- **Refugee acceptance:** Please indicate how strongly you agree or disagree with the following statement: The United States/Tunisia should accept 500 refugees from the conflict hotspot.

Mediators

- **Civilian violence:** In your opinion, to what extent does the Moravian insurgent group use violence against civilians?
- **Gender equality:** To what extent do you think the Moravian insurgent group supports women's equality?
- **Military capacity:** Compared to Falconian state forces, what is your best estimate of Moravian insurgent groups' military capability?
- **Reputation:** Please indicate how strongly you agree or disagree with the following statement. Supporting the Moravian insurgency would be good for the reputation of the United States/Tunisia in the global community.
- **Security interest**: Please indicate how strongly you agree or disagree with the following statement. Supporting the Moravian insurgency would be good for the security interests of the United States/Tunisia.
- **Morally justified:** To what extent do you believe that the Moravian insurgent group's tactic of armed struggle is morally justified?
- **Democratic**: In your opinion, to what extent does the Moravian insurgent group support democratic principles?
- **Repression**: In your opinion, how much repression does the Moravian insurgent group face from its adversary, the Falconian state forces?

A2 Treatments[1]

US Treatment

You will now read a news item about a hypothetical conflict abroad and a situation the United States could face in the future. The situation is general, and is not about a real specific country or group in the news today. We will then ask you a few short questions about the conflict. Please read the following news item carefully. You are going to answer questions based on the information presented here.

Tunisia Treatment

(the Arabic text here reads the same as the English text for the US treatment)

ستقرأ الآن خبرا عن صراع افتراضي في الخارج متمثل في وضعية قد تواجهها تونس في المستقبل. الوضعية عامة، ولا تتعلق بدولة أو مجموعة حقيقية محددة بالذات موجودة في أخبار اليوم. بعد ذلك سنطرح عليك بعض الأسئلة القصيرة حول الصراع.

يرجى قراءة الخبر التالي بعناية و الإجابة على الأسئلة بناءً على المعلومات المقدمة أدناه. إنّ دقة إجاباتك على سؤال فحص الذاكرة ستكون معيارا لتحديد جزء من مكافأتك.

---

[1] Treatments are presented before the outcome and mediator questions in the survey experiment.

منتدى الأخبار

يسعى المتمردون المورافيون للحصول على دعم أجنبي مع تصاعد الصراع

في الأسبوع الماضي، شنّت قوات دولة فالكونيا هجوما بريا على جبهة تحرير مورافيا - الجماعة المتمردة التي تقاتل ضد حكومة فالكونيا منذ عام 2005، في سبيل تأسيس دولة انفصالية اسمها مورافيا داخل فالكونيا. نفّذ متمردو مورافيا (في الصورة أعلاه) يوم أمس عملية انتقامية أسفرت عن مقتل أربعة جنود من فالكونيا على الأقل خلال مراسم عسكرية. مع تصاعد التوترات في المنطقة، يتبادل كلٌّ من حكومة فالكونيا وزعماء المتمردين المورافيين الاتهامات باستهداف المدنيين المستضعفين. وفي مقابلة الأسبوع الماضي، صرّح متمرد من جبهة تحرير مورافيا: "أننا لا نريد الانفصال عن فالكونيا وإقامة دولة جديدة ولكن نريد أن نعيش بحرية على أرضنا داخل حدود فالكونيا، فنحن نناضل من أجل ضمان الحقوق العرقية للمورافيين". تدرس تونس حاليا إمكانية إرسال مساعدات اقتصادية وعسكرية إلى جبهة تحرير مورافيا لدعمها ضد دولة فالكونيا، التي تعتبر خصما لتونس منذ فترة طويلة. يعتقد العديد من الخبراء في تونس أنّ دعم المجموعة المتمردة يتماشى مع المصالح الاستراتيجية التونسية، بينما يرى آخرون أنها ستكون مكلفة للغاية لجانب الدولة التونسية".

Figure A2.1

منتدى الأخبار

يسعى المتمردون المورافيون للحصول على دعم أجنبي مع تصاعد الصراع

في الأسبوع الماضي ، شنّت قوات دولة فالكونيا هجوما بريا على جبهة تحرير مورافيا - الجماعة المتمردة التي تقاتل ضد حكومة فالكونيا منذ عام 2005، في سبيل تأسيس دولة انفصالية اسمها مورافيا داخل فالكونيا. نفّذ متمردو مورافيا (في الصورة أعلاه) يوم أمس عملية انتقامية أسفرت عن مقتل أربعة جنود من فالكونيا على الأقل خلال مراسم عسكرية. مع تصاعد التوترات في المنطقة، يتبادل كلٌّ من حكومة فالكونيا وزعماء المتمردين المورافيين الاتهامات باستهداف المدنيين المستضعفين. وفي مقابلة الأسبوع الماضي، صرّح متمرد من جبهة تحرير مورافيا؛ "أننا لا نريد الانفصال عن فالكونيا وإقامة دولة جديدة ولكن نريد أن نعيش بحرية على أرضنا داخل حدود فالكونيا، فنحن نناضل من أجل ضمان الحقوق العرقية للمورافيين". تدرس تونس حاليا إمكانية إرسال مساعدات اقتصادية وعسكرية إلى جبهة تحرير مورافيا لدعمها ضد دولة فالكونيا، التي تعتبر خصما لتونس منذ فترة طويلة. يعتقد العديد من الخبراء في تونس أنّ دعم المجموعة المتمردة يتماشى مع المصلح الاستراتيجية التونسية، بينما يرى آخرون أنّها ستكون مكلفة للغاية لجانب الدولة التونسية".

Figure A2.2

Moravian Rebels Seek Foreign Support as Conflict Escalates

By Forum News Service on Jan 25, 2024, at 12:02 p.m.

Last week, Falconian state forces launched a ground assault against Moravian Liberation Front– the rebel group who has been fighting against the Falconian government since 2005, for an independent Moravian state within Falconia. Moravian rebels (pictured above) retaliated yesterday, killing at least four Falconian soldiers during a military ceremony.

As tensions escalate in the region, both the Falconian government and Moravian rebel leaders accuse each other of targeting vulnerable civilians. In an interview last week, a rebel from Moravia Liberation Front said, "we don't want to separate from Falconia and set up a state. We want to live within the borders of Falconia, on our own land freely. We are fighting for Moravian ethnic rights."

The US is considering sending economic and military assistance to the Moravian Liberation Front against Falconia, a long-time US adversary. Many experts in the US think supporting the rebel group is in line with the US strategic interests, while others argue that it will be too costly for the US.

Figure A2.3

Figure A2.4

A3 Sample Characteristics

Table A1

Variable	Category	Tunisia	US
Gender	Female	429 (46.28%)	289 (34.40%)
	Male	498 (53.72%)	542 (64.52%)
Age	18–24	183 (19.74%)	19 (2.26%)
	25–34	298 (32.15%)	397 (47.26%)
	35–44	266 (28.69%)	184 (21.90%)
	45–54	114 (12.30%)	107 (12.74%)
	55–64	51 (5.50%)	85 (10.12%)
	65 or older	15 (1.62%)	48 (5.71%)
Education	Elementary school degree	12 (1.29%)	4 (0.48%)
	Secondary school degree	55 (5.93%)	5 (0.60%)
	High school diploma or equivalent	196 (21.14%)	171 (20.36%)
	Bachelor's degree	358 (38.62%)	488 (58.10%)
	Graduate degree (MA, PhD)	306 (33.01%)	172 (20.48%)
My Country Active Role	Yes	632 (68.18%)	334 (39.76%)
	No	295 (31.82%)	506 (60.24%)
Political Ideology	Communist	6 (0.65%)	
	National socialist	33 (3.56%)	
	Left-leaning social liberal	235 (25.35%)	
	Centrist	17 (1.83%)	
	Right-leaning liberal	5 (0.54%)	
	Conservative	124 (13.38%)	
	Islamist	268 (28.91%)	
	Other	30 (3.24%)	
	Do not want to answer	107 (11.54%)	
	Republican		205 (24.40%)
	Republican-leaning		67 (7.98%)
	Independent		178 (21.19%)
	Democrat-leaning		101 (12.02%)
	Democrat		289 (34.40%)
News Following	A couple of times a month or less	267 (28.80%)	77 (9.17%)
	Once a week	78 (8.41%)	124 (14.76%)
	2–3 times a week	176 (18.99%)	239 (28.45%)
	Daily	320 (34.52%)	305 (36.31%)
	Several times a day	86 (9.28%)	95 (11.31%)
Gender Attitudes	Strongly disagree	76 (8.20%)	204 (24.29%)
	Somewhat disagree	186 (20.06%)	107 (12.74%)
	Neither agree nor disagree	246 (26.54%)	147 (17.50%)
	Somewhat agree	291 (31.39%)	217 (25.83%)
	Strongly agree	128 (13.81%)	165 (19.64%)

Table A2 Effects of insurgent gender on foreign public support: US (corresponds to Figure 2)

US	Model 1 Verbal endorsement	Model 2 Verbal endorsement	Model 3 Economic support	Model 4 Economic support	Model 5 Military intervention	Model 6 Military intervention	Model 7 Refugee acceptance	Model 8 Refugee acceptance
Female Combatants	0.237***	0.278***	0.088	0.134*	0.006	0.074	0.153*	0.153*
	(0.088)	(0.079)	(0.091)	(0.077)	(0.098)	(0.075)	(0.090)	(0.083)
Age		−0.059*		−0.108***		−0.268***		−0.182***
		(0.034)		(0.034)		(0.033)		(0.036)
Gender		−0.090		−0.063		0.119		−0.148*
		(0.083)		(0.082)		(0.079)		(0.088)
Education		0.094		0.066		0.075		−0.014
		(0.059)		(0.058)		(0.056)		(0.062)
US active		0.907***		1.160***		1.068***		0.780***
		(0.085)		(0.084)		(0.081)		(0.090)
Ideology		0.061**		0.054**		0.003		0.122***
		(0.026)		(0.026)		(0.025)		(0.028)
News following		−0.015		0.013		−0.080**		0.055
		(0.037)		(0.036)		(0.035)		(0.039)
Gender attitude		0.150***		0.122***		0.303***		−0.085***
		(0.031)		(0.031)		(0.030)		(0.033)
Constant	3.133***	0.885***	3.126***	0.740**	2.811***	0.851***	3.322***	2.404***
	(0.062)	(0.331)	(0.063)	(0.326)	(0.068)	(0.314)	(0.063)	(0.348)
Observations	840	840	840	840	840	840	840	840
R-squared	0.009	0.221	0.001	0.283	0.000	0.425	0.003	0.177

Note: Standard errors in parentheses *** p < 0.01, ** p < 0.05, * p < 0.1.

Table A3 Effects of insurgent gender on foreign public support: Tunisia (corresponds to Figure 3)

TUNISIA	Model 1 Verbal endorsement	Model 2 Verbal endorsement	Model 3 Economic support	Model 4 Economic support	Model 5 Military intervention	Model 6 Military intervention	Model 7 Refugee acceptance	Model 8 Refugee acceptance
Female combatants	0.077	0.072	0.094	0.097	0.089	0.108	0.030	0.029
	(0.072)	(0.071)	(0.076)	(0.075)	(0.071)	(0.067)	(0.083)	(0.081)
Age		−0.066**		−0.134***		−0.197***		−0.118***
		(0.032)		(0.034)		(0.031)		(0.037)
Gender		−0.036		−0.064		−0.002		−0.364***
		(0.079)		(0.083)		(0.075)		(0.090)
Education		−0.062		−0.095**		−0.166***		−0.143***
		(0.039)		(0.040)		(0.036)		(0.044)
Tunisia active		0.185**		0.175**		0.068		0.241***
		(0.077)		(0.080)		(0.073)		(0.088)
Ideology		−0.022		0.007		0.034**		−0.023
		(0.015)		(0.015)		(0.014)		(0.017)
News following		−0.032		−0.026		−0.036		0.004
		(0.027)		(0.028)		(0.026)		(0.031)
Gender attitude		0.038		0.044		0.098***		−0.049
		(0.033)		(0.034)		(0.031)		(0.038)
Constant	2.594***	2.893***	2.411***	2.812***	2.110***	2.750***	2.931***	3.937***
	(0.051)	(0.263)	(0.053)	(0.275)	(0.050)	(0.249)	(0.058)	(0.300)
Observations	927	927	927	927	927	927	927	927
R-squared	0.001	0.022	0.002	0.040	0.002	0.111	0.000	0.047

Note: Standard errors in parentheses *** p<0.01, ** p<0.05, * p<0.1.

Table A4 Heterogeneous treatment effects by respondent gender: US (corresponds to Figure 4)

US	Model 1 Verbal endorsement	Model 2 Verbal endorsement	Model 3 Economic support	Model 4 Economic support	Model 5 Military intervention	Model 6 Military intervention	Model 7 Refugee acceptance	Model 8 Refugee acceptance
Female combatants	0.198*	0.277***	0.061	0.148	−0.078	0.033	0.162	0.175*
	(0.109)	(0.098)	(0.112)	(0.097)	(0.120)	(0.093)	(0.112)	(0.103)
Gender	−0.381***	−0.072	−0.404***	−0.049	−0.581***	0.049	−0.296**	−0.172
	(0.128)	(0.119)	(0.132)	(0.117)	(0.141)	(0.113)	(0.132)	(0.125)
Female combatants* gender	0.061	−0.026	0.041	−0.052	0.214	0.123	−0.073	−0.092
	(0.185)	(0.167)	(0.190)	(0.164)	(0.204)	(0.158)	(0.190)	(0.174)
Age		−0.059*		−0.103***		−0.267***		−0.174***
		(0.035)		(0.034)		(0.033)		(0.036)
Education		0.092		0.066		0.075		−0.014
		(0.060)		(0.059)		(0.057)		(0.062)
US active		0.910***		1.168***		1.062***		0.790***
		(0.086)		(0.085)		(0.082)		(0.090)
Ideology		0.062**		0.054**		0.005		0.123***
		(0.027)		(0.026)		(0.025)		(0.028)
News following		−0.016		0.011		−0.082**		0.057
		(0.037)		(0.036)		(0.035)		(0.039)
Gender attitude		0.149***		0.123***		0.304***		−0.081**
		(0.031)		(0.031)		(0.030)		(0.033)
Constant	3.283***	0.896***	3.279***	0.711**	3.026***	0.882***	3.426***	2.351***
	(0.077)	(0.337)	(0.079)	(0.331)	(0.085)	(0.319)	(0.079)	(0.352)
Observations	831	831	831	831	831	831	831	831
R-squared	0.025	0.217	0.020	0.283	0.027	0.425	0.018	0.183

Note: Standard errors in parentheses *** p < 0.01, ** p < 0.05, * p < 0.1.

Table A5 Heterogeneous treatment effects by respondent gender: Tunisia (corresponds to Figure 5)

TUNISIA	Model 1 Verbal endorsement	Model 2 Verbal endorsement	Model 3 Economic support	Model 4 Economic support	Model 5 Military intervention	Model 6 Military intervention	Model 7 Refugee acceptance	Model 8 Refugee acceptance
Female combatants	0.047	0.049	0.120	0.138	0.171*	0.208**	0.021	0.038
	(0.098)	(0.097)	(0.103)	(0.102)	(0.097)	(0.092)	(0.112)	(0.111)
Gender	−0.069	−0.060	0.001	−0.019	0.108	0.107	−0.305***	−0.354***
	(0.101)	(0.107)	(0.107)	(0.112)	(0.101)	(0.101)	(0.117)	(0.123)
Female combatants* gender	0.067	0.048	−0.057	−0.088	−0.176	−0.217	0.022	−0.019
	(0.144)	(0.143)	(0.152)	(0.150)	(0.142)	(0.135)	(0.165)	(0.164)
Age		−0.066**		−0.134***		−0.197***		−0.118***
		(0.032)		(0.034)		(0.031)		(0.037)
Education		−0.062		−0.096**		−0.169***		−0.143***
		(0.039)		(0.040)		(0.036)		(0.044)
Tunisia active		0.183**		0.177**		0.074		0.241***
		(0.077)		(0.081)		(0.073)		(0.088)
Ideology		−0.022		0.008		0.035**		−0.023
		(0.015)		(0.015)		(0.014)		(0.017)
News following		−0.032		−0.025		−0.034		0.004
		(0.027)		(0.029)		(0.026)		(0.031)
Gender attitude		0.038		0.044		0.099***		−0.049
		(0.033)		(0.034)		(0.031)		(0.038)
Constant	2.625***	2.906***	2.410***	2.788***	2.060***	2.692***	3.072***	3.932***
	(0.069)	(0.266)	(0.073)	(0.278)	(0.068)	(0.251)	(0.079)	(0.303)
Observations	927	927	927	927	927	927	927	927
R-squared	0.002	0.023	0.002	0.040	0.003	0.113	0.014	0.047

Note: Standard errors in parentheses *** p < 0.01, ** p < 0.05, * p < 0.1.

Table A6 Heterogenous treatment effects by respondent gender attitudes: US (corresponds to Figure 6)

US	Model 1 Verbal endorsement	Model 2 Verbal endorsement	Model 3 Economic support	Model 4 Economic support	Model 5 Military intervention	Model 6 Military intervention	Model 7 Refugee acceptance	Model 8 Refugee acceptance
Female combatants	0.199	0.349*	0.045	0.224	−0.116	0.027	0.010	0.115
	(0.197)	(0.182)	(0.204)	(0.179)	(0.201)	(0.173)	(0.208)	(0.191)
Gender attitude	0.198***	0.161***	0.191***	0.137***	0.412***	0.296***	−0.045	−0.091**
	(0.041)	(0.041)	(0.042)	(0.040)	(0.042)	(0.039)	(0.043)	(0.043)
Female comb* gender att.	0.022	−0.023	0.024	−0.030	0.061	0.016	0.046	0.012
	(0.059)	(0.054)	(0.061)	(0.053)	(0.060)	(0.051)	(0.062)	(0.057)
Age		−0.058*		−0.107***		−0.269***		−0.182***
		(0.034)		(0.034)		(0.033)		(0.036)
Gender		−0.089		−0.062		0.119		−0.148*
		(0.083)		(0.082)		(0.079)		(0.088)
Education		0.095		0.067		0.075		−0.014
		(0.059)		(0.058)		(0.056)		(0.062)
US active		0.909***		1.163***		1.066***		0.779***
		(0.086)		(0.084)		(0.081)		(0.090)
Ideology		0.062**		0.054**		0.003		0.122***
		(0.026)		(0.026)		(0.025)		(0.028)
News following		−0.015		0.012		−0.079**		0.056
		(0.037)		(0.036)		(0.035)		(0.039)
Constant	2.517***	0.842**	2.533***	0.685**	1.530***	0.880***	3.462***	2.427***
	(0.140)	(0.346)	(0.145)	(0.340)	(0.143)	(0.329)	(0.148)	(0.364)
Observations	840	840	840	840	840	840	840	840
R-squared	0.066	0.221	0.052	0.284	0.209	0.425	0.005	0.177

Note: Standard errors in parentheses *** p < 0.01, ** p < 0.05, * p < 0.1.

Table A7 Heterogenous treatment effects by respondent gender attitudes: Tunisia (corresponds to Figure 7)

TUNISIA	Model 1 Verbal endorsement	Model 2 Verbal endorsement	Model 3 Economic support	Model 4 Economic support	Model 5 Military intervention	Model 6 Military intervention	Model 7 Refugee acceptance	Model 8 Refugee acceptance
Female combatants	−0.148	−0.154	−0.377*	−0.341	−0.427**	−0.337*	−0.165	−0.199
	(0.211)	(0.211)	(0.222)	(0.220)	(0.208)	(0.199)	(0.245)	(0.241)
Gender attitude	0.012	0.002	−0.013	−0.025	0.033	0.028	−0.014	−0.085
	(0.044)	(0.045)	(0.046)	(0.047)	(0.043)	(0.043)	(0.051)	(0.052)
Female comb* gender att.	0.070	0.070	0.146**	0.136**	0.160***	0.138**	0.060	0.071
	(0.062)	(0.061)	(0.065)	(0.064)	(0.061)	(0.058)	(0.071)	(0.070)
Age		−0.066**		−0.132***		−0.195***		−0.118***
		(0.032)		(0.034)		(0.031)		(0.037)
Gender		−0.037		−0.065		−0.004		−0.365***
		(0.079)		(0.083)		(0.075)		(0.090)
Education		−0.063		−0.097**		−0.168***		−0.144***
		(0.039)		(0.040)		(0.036)		(0.044)
Tunisia active		0.184**		0.174**		0.068		0.241***
		(0.077)		(0.080)		(0.073)		(0.088)
Ideology		−0.023		0.006		0.033**		−0.023
		(0.015)		(0.015)		(0.014)		(0.017)
News following		−0.031		−0.024		−0.034		0.005
		(0.027)		(0.028)		(0.026)		(0.031)
Constant	2.555***	3.013***	2.451***	3.044***	2.002***	2.985***	2.978***	4.058***
	(0.150)	(0.283)	(0.158)	(0.295)	(0.148)	(0.267)	(0.174)	(0.323)
Observations	927	927	927	927	927	927	927	927
R-squared	0.005	0.024	0.011	0.044	0.024	0.116	0.001	0.048

Note: Standard errors in parentheses, *** p<0.01, ** p<0.05, *p<0.1.

Table A8 How are groups with female combatants perceived? The effect of female combatants on potential mechanisms: US (corresponds to Figure 8)

US	Model 1 Civilian violence	Model 2 Civilian violence	Model 3 Morally just	Model 4 Morally just	Model 5 Repression	Model 6 Repression	Model 7 Democratic	Model 8 Democratic	Model 9 Gender equal	Model 10 Gender equal	Model 11 US reputation	Model 12 US reputation	Model 13 Military capacity	Model 14 Military capacity	Model 15 US interests	Model 16 US interests
Female comb.	-0.154**	-0.109*	0.100	0.125*	0.033	0.042	0.190**	0.230***	0.606***	0.638***	0.088	0.130*	-0.110	-0.086	0.080	0.120
	(0.074)	(0.064)	(0.071)	(0.069)	(0.065)	(0.063)	(0.078)	(0.071)	(0.075)	(0.071)	(0.084)	(0.073)	(0.073)	(0.069)	(0.085)	(0.073)
Age		0.144***		-0.054*		-0.042		-0.080***		-0.066**		-0.150***		-0.186***		-0.127***
		(0.028)		(0.030)		(0.027)		(0.031)		(0.031)		(0.032)		(0.030)		(0.032)
Gender		0.045		-0.071		0.069		0.054		-0.081		-0.047		0.156**		-0.080
		(0.068)		(0.073)		(0.067)		(0.075)		(0.075)		(0.077)		(0.073)		(0.078)
Education		0.105**		-0.028		-0.052		0.098*		-0.033		0.124**		0.062		0.087
		(0.049)		(0.052)		(0.047)		(0.053)		(0.054)		(0.055)		(0.052)		(0.055)
US active		0.154**		0.390***		0.365***		0.646***		0.514***		0.877***		-0.099		0.960***
		(0.070)		(0.074)		(0.068)		(0.077)		(0.077)		(0.079)		(0.075)		(0.080)
Ideology		-0.016		0.010		0.082***		0.065***		0.043*		0.013		-0.050**		0.061**
		(0.022)		(0.023)		(0.021)		(0.024)		(0.024)		(0.024)		(0.023)		(0.025)
News		-0.039		0.011		0.021		-0.014		0.056*		-0.030		0.019		-0.022
		(0.076)		(0.032)		(0.029)		(0.033)		(0.033)		(0.034)		(0.032)		(0.034)
Gender att.		0.277***		0.122***		0.061**		0.177***		0.136***		0.145***		0.123***		0.139***
		(0.026)		(0.027)		(0.025)		(0.028)		(0.028)		(0.029)		(0.027)		(0.029)
Constant	3.312***	2.380***	3.448***	2.667***	3.679***	2.878***	3.065***	1.140***	3.233***	2.014***	3.221***	1.383***	2.424***	2.547***	3.226***	1.184***
	(0.052)	(0.271)	(0.050)	(0.288)	(0.046)	(0.264)	(0.055)	(0.298)	(0.053)	(0.298)	(0.059)	(0.307)	(0.051)	(0.292)	(0.060)	(0.308)
Observation	840	840	840	840	813	813	840	840	840	840	840	840	840	840	840	840
R-squared	0.005	0.259	0.002	0.097	0.000	0.076	0.007	0.200	0.072	0.189	0.001	0.266	0.003	0.108	0.001	0.273

Note: Standard errors in parentheses *** $p<0.01$, ** $p<0.05$, * $p<0.1$.

Table A9 How are groups with female combatants perceived? The effect of female combatants on potential mechanisms: Tunisia (corresponds to Figure 9)

TUNISIA	Model 1 Civilian violence	Model 2 Civilian violence	Model 3 Morally just	Model 4 Morally just	Model 5 Repression	Model 6 Repression	Model 7 Democratic	Model 8 Democratic	Model 9 Gender equal	Model 10 Gender equal	Model 11 Tunisia reputation	Model 12 Tunisia reputation	Model 13 Military capacity	Model 14 Military capacity	Model 15 Tunisia interests	Model 16 Tunisia interests
Female comb.	−0.113 (0.075)	−0.114 (0.076)	0.142* (0.073)	0.142* (0.073)	0.070 (0.062)	0.064 (0.062)	0.167** (0.071)	0.165** (0.070)	0.240*** (0.060)	0.240*** (0.060)	0.016 (0.072)	0.029 (0.070)	0.002 (0.064)	0.007 (0.063)	0.037 (0.070)	0.045 (0.069)
Age		−0.020 (0.034)		−0.047 (0.033)		−0.014 (0.028)		−0.083*** (0.032)		−0.057** (0.027)		−0.138*** (0.032)		−0.115*** (0.029)		−0.107*** (0.031)
Gender		0.078 (0.084)		−0.013 (0.081)		0.049 (0.069)		0.054 (0.078)		−0.004 (0.067)		0.017 (0.078)		0.190*** (0.070)		−0.116 (0.076)
Education		0.024 (0.041)		−0.096** (0.040)		0.051 (0.034)		−0.021 (0.038)		−0.026 (0.033)		−0.116*** (0.038)		−0.004 (0.034)		−0.067* (0.037)
Tunisia active		0.030 (0.082)		0.083 (0.079)		0.084 (0.067)		0.112 (0.076)		0.083 (0.065)		−0.003 (0.076)		0.095 (0.068)		0.077 (0.074)
Ideology		−0.008 (0.015)		−0.014 (0.015)		−0.019 (0.013)		−0.020 (0.014)		−0.006 (0.012)		−0.003 (0.014)		0.029** (0.013)		0.023* (0.014)
News		−0.001 (0.029)		0.033 (0.028)		0.057** (0.024)		0.019 (0.027)		−0.000 (0.023)		−0.047* (0.027)		−0.045* (0.024)		−0.022 (0.026)
Gender att.		−0.001 (0.035)		0.042 (0.034)		−0.004 (0.029)		0.049 (0.033)		0.004 (0.028)		0.032 (0.033)		0.025 (0.029)		0.072** (0.032)
Constant	3.340*** (0.053)	3.273*** (0.279)	2.477*** (0.052)	2.732*** (0.270)	3.413*** (0.044)	3.084*** (0.229)	2.310*** (0.050)	2.348*** (0.260)	2.944*** (0.043)	3.109*** (0.223)	2.535*** (0.051)	3.393*** (0.260)	2.327*** (0.045)	2.292*** (0.232)	1.727*** (0.049)	1.906*** (0.253)
Observations	927	927	927	927	927	927	927	927	927	927	927	927	927	927	927	927
R-squared	0.002	0.005	0.004	0.018	0.001	0.018	0.006	0.021	0.017	0.025	0.000	0.046	0.000	0.058	0.000	0.039

Note: Standard errors in parentheses *** p<0.01, ** p<0.05, * p<0.1.

Table A10 Causal mediation analysis: US (corresponds to Figure 10)

US	Civilian violence	Morally just	Repression	Democratic	Gender equal	US reputation	Military capacity	US security interests
VERBAL ENDORSEMENT								
Indirect (ACME)	-0.038*	0.068	0.016	0.123**	0.368***	0.065	-0.006	0.057
	(-0.083, -0.002)	(-0.032, 0.166)	(-0.048, 0.080)	(0.020, 0.227)	(0.269, 0.475)	(-0.062, 0.186)	(-0.023, 0.004)	(-0.066, 0.175)
Direct	0.275***	0.170**	0.242***	0.116	-0.128	0.174***	0.242***	0.182***
	(0.103, 0.445)	(0.023, 0.316)	(0.074, 0.408)	(-0.029, 0.260)	(-0.284, 0.027)	(0.047, 0.300)	(0.067, 0.416)	(0.051, 0.311)
Total	0.237***	0.239***	0.259***	0.239***	0.240***	0.239***	0.237***	0.239***
	(0.065, 0.411)	(0.060, 0.414)	(0.080, 0.438)	(0.061, 0.416)	(0.060, 0.421)	(0.066, 0.422)	(0.064, 0.410)	(0.065, 0.419)
ECONOMIC SUPPORT								
Indirect (ACME)	-0.044**	0.066	0.018	0.124**	0.375***	0.068	-0.01	0.063
	(-0.093, -0.002)	(-0.031, 0.162)	(-0.053, 0.088)	(0.020, 0.230)	(0.274, 0.485)	(0.065, 0.194)	(0.032, 0.004)	(0.072, 0.191)
Direct	0.132	0.024	0.085	-0.034	-0.283***	0.023	0.098	0.028
	(-0.044, 0.306)	(-0.132, 0.177)	(-0.087, 0.255)	(-0.185, 0.115)	(-0.445, -0.124)	(-0.107, 0.151)	(-0.083, 0.276)	(-0.100, 0.153)
Total	0.088	0.09	0.103	0.09	0.092	0.09	0.088	0.09
	(-0.090, 0.268)	(-0.096, 0.272)	(-0.082, 0.288)	(-0.094, 0.273)	(-0.095, 0.277)	(-0.087, 0.278)	(-0.091, 0.267)	(-0.086, 0.277)
MILITARY INTERVENTION								
Indirect (ACME)	-0.091**	0.063	0.017	0.130***	0.372***	0.069	-0.034	0.061
	(-0.187, -0.004)	(-0.029, 0.154)	(-0.050, 0.083)	(0.021, 0.241)	(0.270, 0.483)	(-0.067, 0.199)	(-0.085, 0.011)	(-0.071, 0.187)
Direct	0.098	-0.055	0.012	-0.121	-0.362***	-0.061	0.04	-0.053
	(-0.077, 0.270)	(-0.229, 0.118)	(-0.177, 0.198)	(-0.286, 0.042)	(-0.541, -0.186)	(-0.207, 0.084)	(-0.150, 0.228)	(-0.203, 0.096)
Total	0.007	0.008	0.029	0.009	0.01	0.009	0.007	0.009
	(-0.188, 0.198)	(-0.193, 0.206)	(-0.170, 0.230)	(-0.192, 0.207)	(-0.191, 0.206)	(-0.185, 0.208)	(-0.185, 0.202)	(-0.186, 0.207)

Table A10 (cont.)

US	Civilian violence	Morally just	Repression	Democratic	Gender equal	US reputation	Military capacity	US security interests
REFUGEE ACCEPTANCE								
Indirect (ACME)	−0.025*	0.05	0.015	0.089**	0.289***	0.046	0.007	0.04
	(−0.059, −0.001)	(−0.024, 0.126)	(−0.044, 0.074)	(0.014, 0.169)	(0.206, 0.380)	(−0.044, 0.135)	(−0.003, 0.025)	(−0.045, 0.124)
Direct	0.177*	0.104	0.153*	0.065	−0.133	0.108	0.145	0.115
	(−0.002, 0.354)	(−0.062, 0.268)	(−0.022, 0.326)	(−0.101, 0.229)	(−0.305, 0.036)	(−0.090, 0.294)	(−0.110, 0.401)	(−0.184, 0.185)
Total	0.1526	0.1542	0.168	0.1558	0.1545	0.1522	0.1543	0.1555
	(−0.0263, 0.3298)	(−0.0288, 0.3347)	(−0.0156, 0.3549)	(−0.0256, 0.3396)	(−0.0265, 0.3323)	(−0.0274, 0.3296)	(−0.0307, 0.3357)	(−0.0280, 0.3391)

Note: Standard errors in parentheses *** p<0.01, ** p<0.05, * p<0.1. Mediation analysis was conducted individually on each mediator using Hicks and Tingley (2011). Models are estimated by OLS regression.

Table A11 Causal mediation analysis: Tunisia (corresponds to Figure 11)

TUNISIA	Civilian violence	Morally just	Repression	Democratic	Gender equal	Tunisia reputation	Military capacity	Tunisian security interests
VERBAL ENDORSEMENT								
Indirect (ACME)	0.014	0.061	0.018	0.067	0.080***	0.01	0	0.017
	(−0.004, 0.038)	(−0.004, 0.128)	(−0.015, 0.053)	(0.009, 0.128)	(0.037, 0.129)	(−0.069, 0.085)	(−0.007, 0.007)	(−0.047, 0.079)
Direct	0.063	0.018	0.06	0.012	−0.001	0.069	0.078	0.061
	(−0.078, 0.203)	(−0.111, 0.145)	(−0.079, 0.197)	(−0.120, 0.142)	(−0.139, 0.135)	(−0.053, 0.189)	(−0.065, 0.218)	(−0.066, 0.189)
Total	0.077	0.079	0.078	0.079	0.079	0.079	0.078	0.079
	(−0.066, 0.216)	(−0.067, 0.222)	(−0.064, 0.223)	(−0.065, 0.220)	(−0.064, 0.221)	(−0.066, 0.216)	(−0.064, 0.219)	(−0.066, 0.222)
ECONOMIC SUPPORT								
Indirect (ACME)	0.018	0.059	0.017	0.071***	0.071***	0.011	0	0.018
	(−0.006, 0.049)	(−0.003, 0.124)	(−0.014, 0.051)	(0.032, 0.117)	(0.032, 0.117)	(−0.074, 0.092)	(−0.014, 0.015)	(−0.049, 0.084)
Direct	0.074	0.036	0.077	0.024	0.024	0.084	0.093	0.077
	(−0.074, 0.221)	(−0.103, 0.172)	(−0.071, 0.223)	(−0.124, 0.169)	(−0.124, 0.169)	(−0.043, 0.210)	(−0.057, 0.241)	(−0.060, 0.211)
Total	0.093	0.095	0.094	0.095	0.095	0.095	0.094	0.095
	(−0.056, 0.239)	(−0.057, 0.245)	(−0.057, 0.248)	(−0.055, 0.246)	(−0.057, 0.245)	(−0.057, 0.245)	(−0.056, 0.244)	(−0.058, 0.245)
MILITARY INTERVENTION								
Indirect (ACME)	0.01	0.045	0.011	0.051***	0.044***	0.009	0	0.018
	(−0.003, 0.029)	(−0.003, 0.095)	(−0.009, 0.034)	(0.007, 0.099)	(0.018, 0.077)	(−0.065, 0.080)	(−0.016, 0.018)	(−0.047, 0.081)
Direct	0.079	0.046	0.079	0.039	0.047	0.081	0.089	0.073
	(−0.062, 0.218)	(−0.089, 0.178)	(−0.061, 0.218)	(−0.096, 0.173)	(−0.094, 0.186)	(−0.042, 0.203)	(−0.051, 0.228)	(−0.054, 0.199)
Total	0.089	0.091	0.09	0.091	0.091	0.091	0.09	0.091
	(−0.053, 0.229)	(−0.051, 0.233)	(−0.054, 0.235)	(−0.050, 0.232)	(−0.052, 0.236)	(−0.053, 0.229)	(−0.054, 0.235)	(−0.054, 0.232)

Table A11 (cont.)

TUNISIA	Civilian violence	Morally just	Repression	Democratic	Gender equal	Tunisia reputation	Military capacity	Tunisian security interests
REFUGEE ACCEPTANCE								
Indirect (ACME)	0.014	0.039	0.014	0.050***	0.070***	0.006	−0.001	0.011
	(−0.005, 0.039)	(−0.002, 0.085)	(−0.012, 0.044)	(0.007, 0.099)	(0.031, 0.116)	(−0.040, 0.051)	(−0.016, 0.018)	(−0.031, 0.054)
Direct	0.015	−0.008	0.016	−0.019	−0.038	0.025	0.03	0.019
	(−0.149, 0.177)	(−0.169, 0.150)	(−0.147, 0.177)	(−0.179, 0.139)	(−0.199, 0.122)	(−0.134, 0.182)	(−0.134, 0.192)	(−0.141, 0.177)
Total	0.029	0.031	0.03	0.031	0.031	0.031	0.03	0.031
	(−0.136, 0.191)	(−0.133, 0.198)	(−0.137, 0.200)	(−0.133, 0.199)	(−0.134, 0.199)	(−0.132, 0.198)	(−0.137, 0.192)	(−0.133, 0.198)

Note: Standard errors in parentheses. *** $p < 0.01$, ** $p < 0.05$, * $p < 0.1$. Mediation analysis was conducted individually on each mediator using Hicks and Tingley (2011). Models are estimated by OLS regression.

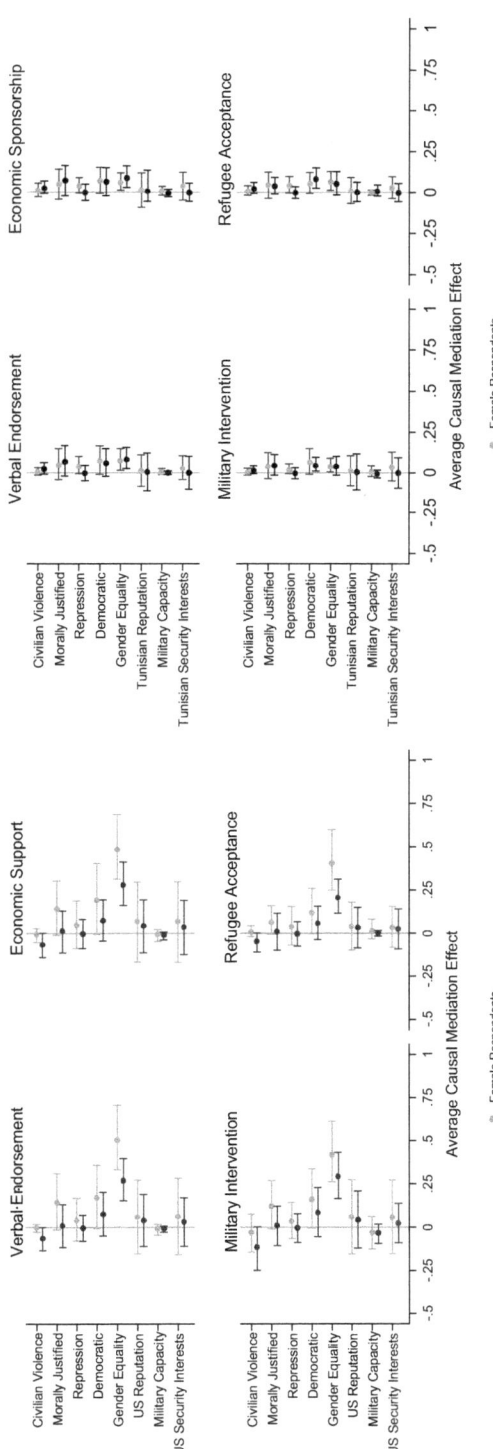

Figures A2.5.1 and A2.5.2 Causal mediation analysis by respondent gender on support index: US (left) and Tunisia (right). Lines represent 95 percent confidence intervals. Models are estimated by OLS regression.

Note: Mediation analysis was conducted individually on each mediator using Hicks and Tingley (2011).

Table A12 Female combatants and democratic support: robustness checks

	Model 1 Democratic support	Model 2 Proportion of democratic support	Model 3 Democratic support	Model 4 Proportion of democratic support	Model 5 Democratic support	Model 6 Proportion of democratic support
Female combatants	0.706*	0.675*	0.164*	0.162**	0.158*	0.150**
	(0.367)	(0.351)	(0.0854)	(0.0714)	(0.0843)	(0.0660)
Conflict duration	0.0558**	0.0395**	0.0169**	0.00816	0.0190**	0.00899*
	(0.0245)	(0.0201)	(0.00844)	(0.00561)	(0.00797)	(0.00501)
Conflict intensity	−0.0406	−0.0541	−0.00892	−0.00852	−0.00809	−0.00919
	(0.0661)	(0.0554)	(0.0186)	(0.00962)	(0.0198)	(0.0101)
Rebel troop size	0.0143***	0.00876*	0.00344***	0.000162	0.00450***	0.00145
	(0.00497)	(0.00451)	(0.00128)	(0.000896)	(0.00127)	(0.00111)
Very weak rebels	0.0566	0.00845	−0.00378	−0.0117		
	(0.308)	(0.347)	(0.0898)	(0.0802)		
Rebel competition	0.00776	0.00811	0.00393	0.00303	0.00146	0.000341
	(0.0395)	(0.0390)	(0.00858)	(0.00636)	(0.00803)	(0.00573)
Forced recruitment	−0.280	−0.208	−0.0572	−0.0483	−0.109	−0.0990
	(0.392)	(0.362)	(0.0937)	(0.0702)	(0.0897)	(0.0675)
Transnational constituencies	0.144	0.0381	0.0636	0.0368		
	(0.168)	(0.165)	(0.0555)	(0.0461)		

Target state regime	−0.0640**	−0.0480*	−0.0162**	−0.00968	−0.0170**	−0.0112*
	(0.0309)	(0.0270)	(0.00790)	(0.00648)	(0.00793)	(0.00586)
Target state power	0.334**	0.337**	0.101***	0.0897***	0.0850***	0.0719***
	(0.132)	(0.142)	(0.0335)	(0.0301)	(0.0276)	(0.0238)
Leftist rebel groups			−0.0326	−0.0686		
			(0.125)	(0.106)		
Islamist rebel groups			−0.172	−0.141		
			(0.124)	(0.0896)		
Constant	0.397		0.673**	0.627**	0.584***	0.526***
	(0.833)		(0.273)	(0.238)	(0.191)	(0.165)
Observations	120	120	118	118	130	130
R-squared	0.293	0.148	0.338	0.284	0.317	0.249

Note: Robust standard errors clustered by conflict in parentheses *** $p < 0.01$, ** $p < 0.05$, * $p < 0.1$.

References

Aaldering, Loes, and Daphne Joanna Van Der Pas. 2020. "Political Leadership in the Media: Gender Bias in Leader Stereotypes during Campaign and Routine Times." *British Journal of Political Science* 50(3): 911–31. https://doi.org/10.1017/S0007123417000795.

Abadi, Jacob. 2017. "Tunisia and Israel: Relations under Stress." *Middle Eastern Studies* 53(4): 507–32. https://doi.org/10.1080/00263206.2016.1263191.

Adams, James, David Bracken, Noam Gidron, Will Horne, Diana Z. O'Brien, and Kaitlin Senk. 2023. "Can't We All Just Get Along? How Women MPs Can Ameliorate Affective Polarization in Western Publics." *American Political Science Review* 117(1): 318–24. https://doi.org/10.1017/S0003055422000491.

Agadullina, Elena R., and Andrey V. Lovakov. 2018. "Are People More Prejudiced towards Groups That Are Perceived as Coherent? A Meta-analysis of the Relationship between Out-Group Entitativity and Prejudice." *British Journal of Social Psychology* 57(4): 703–31.

Akcinaroglu, Seden, and Efe Tokdemir. 2018. "To Instill Fear or Love: Terrorist Groups and the Strategy of Building Reputation." *Conflict Management and Peace Science* 35(4): 355–77. https://doi.org/10.1177/0738894216634292.

Alakoc, Burcu Pinar. 2020. "Femme Fatale: The Lethality of Female Suicide Bombers." *Studies in Conflict and Terrorism* 43(9): 796–814. https://doi.org/10.1080/1057610X.2018.1505685.

Al Chourouk (Sunrise). 2015. "بسبب جهاد النكاح: عراقية تقتل أحد قادة 'داعش'" (Because of Jihad al-Nikah: An Iraqi Woman Kills One of the Leaders of ISIS)." تورس, September 7. www.turess.com/alchourouk/1129375.

Alison, Miranda. 2004. "Women as Agents of Political Violence: Gendering Security." *Security Dialogue* 35(4): 447–63. https://doi.org/10.1177/0967010604049522.

Allansson, Marie, Erik Melander, and Lotta Themnér. 2017. "Organized Violence, 1989–2016." *Journal of Peace Research* 54(4): 574–87. https://doi.org/10.1177/0022343317718773.

Amwaj Media. 2021. "Kuwait Allows Women to Join Military, Igniting Debate." October 19. https://amwaj.media/en/media-monitor/kuwait-allows-women-to-join-military-igniting-debate-among-citizens.

Angrist, Joshua D., and Jörn-Steffen Pischke. 2008. *Mostly Harmless Econometrics: An Empiricist's Companion*. Princeton University Press. https://doi.org/10.1515/9781400829828.

Arves, Stephen, Kathleen Gallagher Cunningham, and Caitlin McCulloch. 2019. "Rebel Tactics and External Public Opinion." *Research and Politics* 6(3): 1–7. https://doi.org/10.1177/2053168019877032.

Aydin, Aysegul. 2010. "Where Do States Go? Strategy in Civil War Intervention." *Conflict Management and Peace Science* 27(1): 47–66. https://doi.org/10.1177/0738894209352128.

Balch-Lindsay, Dylan, Andrew J. Enterline, and Kyle A. Joyce. 2008. "Third-Party Intervention and the Civil War Process." *Journal of Peace Research* 45(3): 345–63. https://doi.org/10.1177/0022343308088815.

Barnard, Anne. 2011. "Libya's War-Tested Women Hope to Keep New Power." *New York Times*, September 12. www.nytimes.com/2011/09/13/world/africa/13women.html.

Barnes, Tiffany D., and Emily Beaulieu. 2014. "Gender Stereotypes and Corruption: How Candidates Affect Perceptions of Election Fraud." *Politics & Gender* 10(3): 365–91. https://doi.org/10.1017/s1743923x14000221.

Barnes, Tiffany D., and Emily Beaulieu. 2019. "Women Politicians, Institutions, and Perceptions of Corruption." *Comparative Political Studies* 52(1): 134–67. https://doi.org/10.1177/0010414018774355.

Barnes, Tiffany D., and Diana Z. O'Brien. 2018. "Defending the Realm: The Appointment of Female Defense Ministers Worldwide." *American Journal of Political Science* 62(2): 355–68. https://doi.org/10.1111/ajps.12337.

Barrios Sabogal, Laura Camila. 2021. "Beyond Victimization: Agency of Former Female FARC-EP Combatants in Colombia." *Zeitschrift Für Friedens- Und Konfliktforschung* 10(1): 83–101. https://doi.org/10.1007/s42597-020-00054-w.

Başer, Caglayan. 2022. "Women Insurgents, Rebel Organization Structure, and Sustaining the Rebellion: The Case of the Kurdistan Workers' Party." *Security Studies* 31(3): 381–416. https://doi.org/10.1080/09636412.2022.2097889.

Baum, Matthew A., and Philip B. K. Potter. 2008. "The Relationships between Mass Media, Public Opinion, and Foreign Policy: Toward a Theoretical Synthesis." *Annual Review of Political Science* 11: 39–65. https://doi.org/10.1146/annurev.polisci.11.060406.214132.

Baum, Matthew A., and Philip B. K. Potter. 2015. *War and Democratic Constraint: How the Public Influences Foreign Policy*. Princeton University Press. https://doi.org/10.1515/9781400866472.

BBC. 2016. "Female Front Line Soldiers 'Will Put Lives at Risk', Says Ex-Army Chief." *BBC News*, April 6. www.bbc.com/news/uk-politics-35976113.

Ben-Shitrit, Lihi, Julia Elad-Strenger, and Sivan Hirsch-Hoefler. 2022. "'Pinkwashing' the Radical-Right: Gender and the Mainstreaming of

Radical-Right Policies and Actions." *European Journal of Political Research* 61(1): 86–110. https://doi.org/10.1111/1475-6765.12442.

Blackman, Alexandra Domike, and Marlette Jackson. 2021. "Gender Stereotypes, Political Leadership, and Voting Behavior in Tunisia." *Political Behavior* 43(3): 1037–66. https://doi.org/10.1007/s11109-019-09582-5.

Bob, Clifford. 2005. *The Marketing of Rebellion: Insurgents, Media, and International Activism*. Cambridge University Press. https://doi.org/10.1017/CBO9780511756245.

Boutron, Camille. 2017. "Colombian Militants Have a New Plan for the Country, and It's Called 'Insurgent Feminism.'" *The Conversation*, July 3, 2017.

Braithwaite, Alex, and Luna B. Ruiz. 2018. "Female Combatants, Forced Recruitment, and Civil Conflict Outcomes." *Research and Politics* 5(2): 1–7. https://doi.org/10.1177/2053168018770559.

Brannon, Elizabeth. 2023. "Celebrated and Sidelined: How Women's Roles in the National Resistance Army Shaped Post-Conflict Gender Politics." *Civil Wars* 27(1): 165–88. https://doi.org/10.1080/13698249.2023.2230812.

Brannon, Elizabeth L., and Jakana Thomas. forthcoming. *Legislating Peace: How Gender Diverse Rebel Parties Encourage the Implementation of Gender Peace Agreement Provisions*. Elements in Gender and Politics. Cambridge University Press.

Brooks, Deborah Jordan, and Benjamin A. Valentino. 2011. "A War of One's Own: Understanding the Gender Gap in Support for War." *Public Opinion Quarterly* 75(2): 270–86. https://doi.org/10.1093/poq/nfr005.

Brun, Cathrine. 2005. "Women in the Local/Global Fields of War and Displacement in Sri Lanka." *Gender, Technology and Development* 9(1): 57–80. https://doi.org/10.1177/097185240500900104.

Brutger, Ryan, Joshua D. Kertzer, Jonathan Renshon, Dustin Tingle, and Chagai M. Weiss. 2023. "Abstraction and Detail in Experimental Design." *American Journal of Political Science* 67(4): 979–95. https://doi.org/10.1111/ajps.12710.

Bush, Sarah Sunn, and Pär Zetterberg. 2021. "Gender Quotas and International Reputation." *American Journal of Political Science* 65(2): 326–41. https://doi.org/10.1111/ajps.12557.

Bush, Sarah Sunn, Daniela Donno, and Pär Zetterberg. 2024. "International Rewards for Gender Equality Reforms in Autocracies." *American Political Science Review* 118(3): 1189–203. https://doi.org/10.1017/S0003055423001016.

Campbell, Donald T. 1958. "Common Fate, Similarity, and Other Indices of the Status of Aggregates of Persons as Social Entities." *Behavioral Science* 3(1): 14–25. https://doi.org/10.1002/bs.3830030103.

Caprioli, Mary, and Mark A. Boyer. 2001. "Gender, Violence, and International Crisis." *Journal of Conflict Resolution* 45(4): 503–18. https://doi.org/10.1177/0022002701045004005.

Carpenter, R. Charli. 2005. "Women, Children and Other Vulnerable Groups: Gender, Strategic Frames and the Protection of Civilians as a Transnational Issue." *International Studies Quarterly*, 49(2): 295–334.

Caspersen, Nina. 2009. "Playing the Recognition Game: External Actors and De Facto States." *International Spectator* 44(4): 47–60. https://doi.org/10.1080/03932720903351146.

Chaudoin, Stephen, Brian J. Gaines, and Avital Livny. 2021. "Survey Design, Order Effects, and Causal Mediation Analysis." *Journal of Politics* 83(4): 1851–6. https://doi.org/10.1086/715166.

Chu, Jonathan A. 2021. "Liberal Ideology and Foreign Opinion on China." *International Studies Quarterly* 65(4): 960–72. https://doi.org/10.1093/isq/sqab062.

Chu, Jonathan A., and Stefano Recchia. 2022. "Does Public Opinion Affect the Preferences of Foreign Policy Leaders? Experimental Evidence from the UK Parliament." *Journal of Politics* 84(3): 1874–7. https://doi.org/10.1086/719007.

Clayton, Amanda, Diana Z. O'Brien, and Jennifer M. Piscopo. 2019. "All Male Panels? Representation and Democratic Legitimacy." *American Journal of Political Science* 63(1): 113–29. https://doi.org/10.1111/ajps.12391.

Clifford, Scott, Ryan M. Jewell, and Philip D. Waggoner. 2015. "Are Samples Drawn from Mechanical Turk Valid for Research on Political Ideology?" *Research and Politics* 2(4): 1–9. https://doi.org/10.1177/2053168015622072.

Cohen, Dara Kay. 2013. "Explaining Rape during Civil War: Cross-National Evidence (1980–2009)." *American Political Science Review* 107(3): 461–77.

Cohen, Dara Kay, and Sabrina M. Karim. 2022. "Does More Equality for Women Mean Less War? Rethinking Sex and Gender Inequality and Political Violence." *International Organization* 76(2): 414–44. https://doi.org/10.1017/S0020818321000333.

Conover, Pamela Johnston, and Virginia Sapiro. 1993. "Gender, Feminist Consciousness, and War." *American Journal of Political Science* 37(4): 1079–99. https://doi.org/10.2307/2111544.

Crawford, Matthew T., Steven J. Sherman, and David L. Hamilton. 2002. "Perceived Entitativity, Stereotype Formation, and the Interchangeability of

Group Members." *Journal of Personality and Social Psychology* 83(5): 1076–94. https://doi.org/10.1037//0022-3514.83.5.1076.

Cunningham, David E., Kristian Skrede Gleditsch, and Idean Salehyan. 2009. "It Takes Two: A Dyadic Analysis of Civil War Duration and Outcome." *Journal of Conflict Resolution* 53(4): 570–97. https://doi.org/10.1177/0022002709336458.

Darden, Jessica Trisko, Alexis Henshaw, and Ora Szekely. 2019. *Insurgent Women: Female Combatants in Civil Wars*. Georgetown University Press.

Demeritt, Jacqueline H. R., Angela D. Nichols, and Eliza G. Kelly. 2014. "Female Participation and Civil War Relapse." *Civil Wars* 16(3): 346–68. https://doi.org/10.1080/13698249.2014.966427.

Dietrich, Simone, Daniela Donno, Katharina Fleiner, and Alice Iannantuoni. 2025. "The Politics of Gender Mainstreaming in Foreign Aid." *International Studies Quarterly* 69(2): sqaf033. https://doi.org/10.1093/isq/sqaf033.

Dill, Janina, Scott D. Sagan, and Benjamin A. Valentino. 2022. "Kettles of Hawks: Public Opinion on the Nuclear Taboo and Noncombatant Immunity in the United States, United Kingdom, France, and Israel." *Security Studies* 31(1): 1–31. https://doi.org/10.1080/09636412.2022.2038663.

Dolan, Kathleen. 2010. "The Impact of Gender Stereotyped Evaluations on Support for Women Candidates." *Political Behavior* 32(1): 69–88. https://doi.org/10.1007/s11109-009-9090-4.

Donald, Heather Mac. 2019. "Women Don't Belong in Combat Units." *Wall Street Journal*, January 13.

Dovi, Suzanne. 2007. "Theorizing Women's Representation in the United States." *Politics and Gender* 3(3): 297–319. https://doi.org/10.1017/S1743923X07000281.

Edgell, Amanda B. 2017. "Foreign Aid, Democracy, and Gender Quota Laws." *Democratization* 24(6): 1103–41. https://doi.org/10.1080/13510347.2016.1278209.

Eichenberg, Richard C. 2003. "Gender Differences in Public Attitudes toward the Use of Force by the United States, 1990–2003." *International Security* 28(1): 110–41. (Reprinted in Bruce Russett (ed.), *International Security and Conflict*, Routledge: [Ashgate, 2008] 2016, pp. 413–44.)

Eichenberg, Richard C. 2005. "Victory Has Many Friends: US Public Opinion and the Use of Military Force, 1981–2005." *International Security* 30(1): 140–77. https://doi.org/10.1162/0162288054894616.

Eichenberg, Richard C. 2016. "Gender Difference in American Public Opinion on the Use of Military Force, 1982–2013." *International Studies Quarterly* 60(1): 138–48. https://doi.org/10.1093/isq/sqv019.

Entman, Robert M. 2003. *Projections of Power: Framing News, Public Opinion, and US Foreign Policy*. University of Chicago Press.

Fearon, James D. 1994. "Domestic Political Audiences and the Escalation of International Disputes." *American Political Science Review* 88(3): 577–92. https://doi.org/10.2307/2944796.

Fischer, Bryan. 2019. "Women Absolutely Do Not Belong in Combat." American Family Association. January 22. www.afa.net/the-stand/culture/2019/01/women-absolutely-do-not-belong-in-combat/.

Flanagin, Jake. 2014. "Women Fight ISIS and Sexism in Kurdish Regions." Op-Talk, October 13. https://archive.nytimes.com/op-talk.blogs.nytimes.com/2014/10/13/women-fight-isis-and-sexism-in-kurdish-regions/.

Flock, Elizabeth. 2024. "Inside the Feminist Revolution in Northern Syria." *Noēma*, March 25. www.noemamag.com/inside-the-feminist-revolution-in-northern-syria.

Gadarian, Shana Kushner. 2010. "The Politics of Threat: How Terrorism News Shapes Foreign Policy Attitudes." *Journal of Politics* 72(2): 469–83. https://doi.org/10.1017/S0022381609990910.

Gartner, Scott Sigmund. 2008. "The Multiple Effects of Casualties on Public Support for War: An Experimental Approach." *American Political Science Review* 102(1): 95–106. https://doi.org/10.1017/S0003055408080027.

Gelpi, Christopher, Peter D. Feaver, and Jason Reifler. 2009. *Paying the Human Costs of War: American Public Opinion and Casualties in Military Conflicts*. Princeton University Press. https://doi.org/10.1515/9781400830091.

Gentry, Caron E., and Laura Sjoberg. 2015. *Beyond Mothers, Monsters, Whores: Thinking About Women's Violence in Global Politics*. Bloomsbury Publishing.

Ghiles-Meilhac, Samuel. 2014. "Tunisia's Relations with Israel in a Comparative Approach." *Bulletin Du Centre de Recherche Français à Jérusalem* 25 (November). https://journals.openedition.org/bcrfj/7352.

Giri, Keshab. 2023. "Rebel Governance of Marriage and Sexuality: An Intersectional Approach." *International Studies Quarterly* 67(2): 1–12. https://doi.org/10.1093/isq/sqad028.

Giri, Keshab, and Roos Haer. 2024. "Female Combatants and Durability of Civil War." *Studies in Conflict and Terrorism* 47(5): 526–47. https://doi.org/10.1080/1057610X.2021.1980982.

Goldsmith, Benjamin E., and Yusaku Horiuchi. 2012. "In Search of Soft Power: Does Foreign Public Opinion Matter for US Foreign Policy?" *World Politics* 64(3): 555–85. https://doi.org/10.1017/S0043887112000123.

Goldstein, Joshua S. 2001. *War and Gender: How Gender Shapes the War System and Vice Versa*. Cambridge University Press.

Griffin, Elizabeth. 2014. "YPJ Soliders Fighting ISIS – Women Soldiers in a War Against ISIS. *Marie Claire*, October 1. www.marieclaire.com/culture/news/a6643/these-are-the-women-battling-isis/.

Hamilton, David L., and Steven J. Sherman. 1996. "Perceiving Persons and Groups." *Psychological Review* 103(2): 336–55. https://doi.org/10.1037/0033-295X.103.2.336.

Harbom, Lotta, Erik Melander, and Peter Wallensteen. 2008. "Dyadic Dimensions of Armed Conflict, 1946–2007." *Journal of Peace Research* 45(5): 697–710. https://doi.org/10.1177/0022343308094331.

Harrell, Baylee. 2023. "Can't Live with Them or Can't Live without Them? How Varying Roles of Women in Rebel Groups Influence One-Sided Violence." *International Interactions* 49(6): 875–903. https://doi.org/10.1080/03050629.2023.2233677.

Heger, Lindsay, and Idean Salehyan. 2007. "Ruthless Rulers: Coalition Size and the Severity of Civil Conflict." *International Studies Quarterly* 51(2): 385–403. https://doi.org/10.1111/j.1468-2478.2007.00456.x.

Heilman, Madeline E. 2001. "Description and Prescription: How Gender Stereotypes Prevent Women's Ascent Up the Organizational Ladder." *Journal of Social Issues* 57(4): 657–74. https://doi.org/10.1111/0022-4537.00234.

Heilman, Madeline E., and Michelle C. Haynes. 2005. "No Credit Where Credit Is Due: Attributional Rationalization of Women's Success in Male-Female Teams." *Journal of Applied Psychology* 90(5): 905–16. https://doi.org/10.1037/0021-9010.90.5.905.

Herrera, Natalia, and Douglas Porch. 2008. "'Like Going to a Fiesta' – the Role of Female Fighters in Colombia's FARC-EP." *Small Wars and Insurgencies* 19(4): 609–34. https://doi.org/10.1080/09592310802462547.

Hicks, Raymond, and Dustin Tingley. 2011. "Causal Mediation Analysis." *Stata Journal* 11(4): 605–19. https://doi.org/10.1177/1536867x1101100407.

Hildebrandt, Timothy, Courtney Hillebrecht, Peter M. Holm, and Jon Pevehouse. 2013. "The Domestic Politics of Humanitarian Intervention: Public Opinion, Partisanship, and Ideology." *Foreign Policy Analysis* 9(3): 243–66. https://doi.org/10.1111/j.1743-8594.2012.00189.x.

Holman, Mirya R., Jennifer L. Merolla, and Elizabeth J. Zechmeister. 2011. "Sex, Stereotypes, and Security: A Study of the Effects of Terrorist Threat on Assessments of Female Leadership." *Journal of Women, Politics and Policy* 32(3): 173–92. https://doi.org/10.1080/1554477X.2011.589283.

Holsti, Ole R. 1992. "Public Opinion and Foreign Policy: Challenges to the Almond-Lippmann Consensus." *International Studies Quarterly* 36(4): 439–66. https://doi.org/10.2307/2600734.

Holsti, Ole R. 2004. *Public Opinion and American Foreign Policy*, revised ed. University of Michigan Press. https://doi.org/10.3998/mpub.6750.

Horton, Alex. 2017. "A Bullet Almost Killed This Kurdish Sniper. Then She Laughed About It." *Washington Post*, June 28. www.washingtonpost.com/news/checkpoint/wp/2017/06/28/a-bullet-almost-killed-this-kurdish-sniper-then-she-laughed-about-it/.

Huang, Reyko. 2016. "Rebel Diplomacy in Civil War." *International Security* 40(4): 89–126. https://doi.org/10.1162/ISEC_a_00237.

Hudson, Valerie M., Mary Caprioli, Bonnie Ballif-Spanvill, Rose McDermott, and Chad F. Emmett. 2009. "The Heart of the Matter: The Security of Women and the Security of States." *International Security* 33(3): 7–45. https://doi.org/10.1162/isec.2009.33.3.7.

Hurka, Thomas. 2005. "Proportionality in the Morality of War." *Philosophy and Public Affairs* 33(1): 34–66. https://doi.org/10.1111/j.1088-4963.2005.00024.x.

Imai, Kosuke, Luke Keele, Dustin Tingley, and Teppei Yamamoto. 2011. "Unpacking the Black Box of Causality: Learning About Causal Mechanisms from Experimental and Observational Studies." *American Political Science Review* 105(4): 765–89. https://doi.org/10.1017/S0003055411000414.

Ives, Brandon. 2021. "Ethnic External Support and Rebel Group Splintering." *Terrorism and Political Violence* 33(7): 1546–66. https://doi.org/10.1080/09546553.2019.1636035.

Iyengar, Shanto. 1991. *Is Anyone Responsible? How Television Frames Political Issues*. University of Chicago Press.

Jo, Hyeran. 2015. *Compliant Rebels*. Cambridge University Press.

Jo, Hyeran, Joowon Yi, and Josiah Barrett. 2025. "Humanitarian Rebels? Rebel Governance and International Humanitarian Engagement." *International Politics* 62: 336–57. https://doi.org/10.1057/s41311-023-00521-0.

Jung, Jae-Hee, and Margit Tavits. 2024. *Counter-Stereotypes and Attitudes toward Gender and LGBTQ Equality*. Cambridge University Press.

Kahn, Kim Fridkin. 1996. *The Political Consequences of Being a Woman: How Stereotypes Influence the Conduct and Consequences of Political Campaigns*. Columbia University Press.

Kalyvas, Stathis N. 2003. "The Ontology of 'Political Violence': Action and Identity in Civil Wars." *Perspectives on Politics* 1(3): 475–94. https://doi.org/10.1017/S1537592703000355.

Kao, Kristen, Ellen Lust, Marwa Shalaby, and Chagai M. Weiss. 2024. "Female Representation and Legitimacy: Evidence from a Harmonized Experiment in Jordan, Morocco, and Tunisia." *American Political Science Review* 118(1): 495–503. https://doi.org/10.1017/s0003055423000357.

Kertzer, Joshua D., and Thomas Zeitzoff. 2017. "A Bottom-Up Theory of Public Opinion About Foreign Policy." *American Journal of Political Science* 61(3): 543–58. https://doi.org/10.1111/ajps.12314.

Kertzer, Joshua D., Kathleen E. Powers, Brian C. Rathbun, and Ravi Iyer. 2014. "Moral Support: How Moral Values Shape Foreign Policy Attitudes." *Journal of Politics* 76(3): 825–40. https://doi.org/10.1017/S0022381614000073.

Kollárová, Marta. 2015. "Good or Bad Agents? Western Fascination with Women and the Construction of Female Objects during the ISIS Crisis." Master's thesis, Central European University, Budapest.

Krebs, Ronald R., and Patrick Thaddeus Jackson. 2007. "Twisting Tongues and Twisting Arms: The Power of Political Rhetoric." *European Journal of International Relations* 13(1): 35–66. https://doi.org/10.1177/1354066107074284.

Kreft, Anne-Kathrin, and Mattias Agerberg. 2024. "Imperfect Victims? Civilian Men, Vulnerability, and Policy Preferences." *American Political Science Review* 118(1): 274–90. https://doi.org/10.1017/S0003055423000345.

Kreps, Sarah, and Sarah Maxey. 2018. "Mechanisms of Morality: Sources of Support for Humanitarian Intervention." *Journal of Conflict Resolution* 62(8): 1814–42. https://doi.org/10.1177/0022002717704890.

Krook, Mona Lena, and Diana Z. O'Brien. 2012. "All the President's Men? The Appointment of Female Cabinet Ministers Worldwide." *Journal of Politics* 74(3): 840–55. https://doi.org/10.1017/S0022381612000382.

Kubovich, Yaniv. 2021. "IDF Chief Rabbi Attended Meeting on Women in Combat Roles Despite Army Promise." *Haaretz*, March 3. www.haaretz.com/israel-news/2021-03-03/ty-article/.premium/idf-chief-rabbi-attended-meeting-on-women-in-combat-roles-despite-army-promise/0000017f-db34-d856-a37f-fff467fb0000.

Lawless, Jennifer L. 2004. "Women, War, and Winning Elections: Gender Stereotyping in the Post-September 11th Era." *Political Research Quarterly* 57(3): 479–90. https://doi.org/10.1177/106591290405700312.

Lazarus, Sarah. 2019. "Women. Life. Freedom. Female Fighters of Kurdistan." *CNN*, January 28. www.cnn.com/2019/01/27/homepage2/kurdish-female-fighters/index.html.

Li, Xiaojun, and Dingding Chen. 2021. "Public Opinion, International Reputation, and Audience Costs in an Authoritarian Regime." *Conflict Management and Peace Science* 38(5): 543–60. https://doi.org/10.1177/0738894220906374.

Lin-Greenberg, Erik. 2021. "Soldiers, Pollsters, and International Crises: Public Opinion and the Military's Advice on the Use of Force." *Foreign Policy Analysis* 17(3): 1–12. https://doi.org/10.1093/fpa/orab009.

Liu, Shan-Jan Sarah. 2018. "Are Female Political Leaders Role Models? Lessons from Asia." *Political Research Quarterly* 71(2): 255–69. https://doi.org/10.1177/1065912917745162.

Logan, Carolyn J. 1996. "U.S. Public Opinion and the Intervention in Somalia: Lessons for the Future of Military-Humanitarian Interventions." *Fletcher Forum of World Affairs* 20(2): 155–80.

Loken, Meredith. 2017. "Rethinking Rape: The Role of Women in Wartime Violence." *Security Studies* 26(1): 60–92. https://doi.org/10.1080/09636412.2017.1243915.

Loken, Meredith. 2021. "'Both Needed and Threatened': Armed Mothers in Militant Visuals." *Security Dialogue* 52(1): 21–44. https://doi.org/10.1177/0967010620903237.

Loken, Meredith. 2024. *Women, Gender, and Rebel Governance during Civil Wars*. Elements in Gender and Politics. Cambridge University Press.

Loken, Meredith, and Hilary Matfess. 2024. "Introducing the Women's Activities in Armed Rebellion (WAAR) Project, 1946–2015." *Journal of Peace Research* 61(3): 489–99. https://doi.org/10.1177/00223433221128340.

Lupu, Yonatan, and Geoffrey P. R. Wallace. 2024. "The Laws of War and Public Support for Foreign Combatants." *International Organization* 78(4): 823–52. https://doi.org/10.1017/S0020818324000274.

Lust, Ellen, and Lindsay J. Benstead. 2024. "Is the Future Female? Lessons from a Conjoint Experiment on Voter Preferences in Six Arab Countries." *Comparative Political Studies* 57(14): 2376–413. https://doi.org/10.1177/00104140241237462.

Macdonald, Myra. 2006. "Muslim Women and the Veil: Problems of Image and Voice in Media Representations." *Feminist Media Studies* 6(1): 7–23. https://doi.org/10.1080/14680770500471004.

MacKenzie, Megan. 2009. "Securitization and Desecuritization: Female Soldiers and the Reconstruction of Women in Post-Conflict Sierra Leone." *Security Studies* 18(2): 241–61. https://doi.org/10.1080/09636410902900061.

Manekin, Devorah, and Reed M. Wood. 2020. "Framing the Narrative: Female Fighters, External Audience Attitudes, and Transnational Support for Armed Rebellions." *Journal of Conflict Resolution* 64(9): 1638–65. https://doi.org/10.1177/0022002720912823.

Marshall, Monty, Ted Gurr, and Keith Jaggers. 2017. *Polity™ IV Project – Political Regime Characteristics and Transitions, 1800–2017: Dataset Users' Manual*. Center for Systemic Peace. www.systemicpeace.org/inscr/p4manualv2017.pdf.

Matfess, Hilary. 2024. *In Love and at War: Marriage in Non-state Armed Groups*. Cambridge University Press. https://doi.org/10.1017/9781009358859.

Matfess, Hilary, and Meredith Loken. 2024. "Women's Wings in Rebel Organisations: Prevalence, Purposes and Variations." *Civil Wars* 27(1): 15–41. https://doi.org/10.1080/13698249.2024.2302737.

Mattiacci, Eleonora, and Benjamin T. Jones. 2020. "Restoring Legitimacy: Public Diplomacy Campaigns during Civil Wars." *International Studies Quarterly* 64(4): 867–78. https://doi.org/10.1093/isq/sqaa065.

Mattingly, Daniel C., and James Sundquist. 2023. "When Does Public Diplomacy Work? Evidence from China's 'Wolf Warrior' Diplomats." *Political Science Research and Methods* 11(4): 921–9. https://doi.org/10.1017/psrm.2022.41.

Maxey, Sarah. 2020. "The Power of Humanitarian Narratives: A Domestic Coalition Theory of Justifications for Military Action." *Political Research Quarterly* 73(3): 680–95. https://doi.org/10.1177/1065912919852169.

Mazurana, Dyan E., Susan A. McKay, Khristopher C. Carlson, and Janel C. Kasper. 2002. "Girls in Fighting Forces and Groups: Their Recruitment, Participation, Demobilization, and Reintegration." *Peace and Conflict: Journal of Peace Psychology* 8(2): 97–123. https://doi.org/10.1207/S15327949PAC0802_01.

McDermott, Rose, and Jonathan A. Cowden. 2001. "The Effects of Uncertainty and Sex in a Crisis Simulation Game." *International Interactions* 27(4): 353–80. https://doi.org/10.1080/03050620108434990.

McManus, Anne-Marie. 2013. "Sentimental Terror Narratives: Gendering Violence, Dividing Sympathy." *Journal of Middle East Women's Studies* 9(2): 80–107. https://doi.org/10.2979/jmiddeastwomstud.9.2.80.

Mehrl, Marius. 2022. "Female Combatants and Wartime Rape: Reconsidering the Role of Women in Armed Conflict." *Armed Forces and Society* 48(2): 464–79. https://doi.org/10.1177/0095327x20981696.

Melander, Erik. 2005. "Gender Equality and Intrastate Armed Conflict." *International Studies Quarterly* 49(4): 695–714. https://doi.org/10.1111/j.1468-2478.2005.00384.x.

Mercer, Jonathan. 2010. "Emotional Beliefs." *International Organization* 64(1): 1–31. https://doi.org/10.1017/S0020818309990221.

Meyer-Parlapanis, Danie, Roland Weierstall, Corina Nandi, Manassé Bambonyé, Thomas Elbert, and Anselm Crombach. 2016. "Appetitive Aggression in Women: Comparing Male and Female War Combatants." *Frontiers in Psychology* 6: 1972. https://doi.org/10.3389/fpsyg.2015.01972.

Mishra, A. K. 2024. "Fostering Local Economic Development through Agripreneurship in Nepal." *SAIM Journal of Social Science and Technology* 1(1): 1–11.

Nacos, Brigitte L. 2005. "The Portrayal of Female Terrorists in the Media: Similar Framing Patterns in the News Coverage of Women in Politics and in Terrorism." *Studies in Conflict and Terrorism* 28(5): 435–51. https://doi.org/10.1080/10576100500180352.

Naurin, Daniel, Elin Naurin, and Amy Alexander. 2019 "Gender Stereotyping and Chivalry in International Negotiations: A Survey Experiment in the Council of the European Union." *International Organization* 73(2): 469–88. https://doi.org/10.1017/s0020818319000043.

NBC News. 2024. "Trump's Pick for Defense Secretary Doesn't Want Women Serving in Combat." *NBC*, November 14.

O'Brien, Diana Z. 2019. "Female Leaders and Citizens' Perceptions of Political Parties." *Journal of Elections, Public Opinion and Parties* 29(4): 465–89. https://doi.org/10.1080/17457289.2019.1669612.

O'Rourke, Lindsey A. 2009. "What's Special About Female Suicide Terrorism?" *Security Studies* 18(4): 681–718. https://doi.org/10.1080/09636410903369084.

Ortega, Luisa Maria Dietrich. 2010. *Transitional Justice and Female Ex-combatants: Lessons Learned from International Experience*. Research Brief. International Center for Transitional Justice. www.peacewomen.org/sites/default/files/ddr_femaleexcombatants_0.pdf.

Pasha-Robinson, Lucy. 2017. "Female Yemeni Fighters Carry Babies and Machine Guns at Anti-Saudi Rally." *The Independent*, January 18. www.independent.co.uk/news/world/middle-east/yemen-female-fighters-conflict-huthi-rebels-antisaudi-coalition-rally-sanaa-a7532486.html.

Peez, Anton, and Felix S. Bethke. 2025. "Does Public Opinion on Foreign Policy Affect Elite Preferences? Evidence from the 2022 US Sanctions Against Russia." *International Studies Quarterly* 69(1): sqae145. https://doi.org/10.1093/isq/sqae145.

Peterson, V. Spike. 1992. *Gendered States: Feminist (Re)visions of International Relations Theory*. Lynne Rienner Publishers. https://doi.org/10.1515/9781685859305.

PKK. 1999. Serxwebûn. July: 1.

PKK. 2001. Serxwebûn. August: 7.

PKK. 2023. Serxwebûn. January: 6.

Popkin, Samuel L. 1994. *The Reasoning Voter: Communication and Persuasion in Presidential Campaigns*. University of Chicago Press.

Rajan, V. G. Julie. 2011. *Women Suicide Bombers: Narratives of Violence*. Routledge. https://doi.org/10.4324/9780203821831.

Regan, Patrick M. 2002. "Third-Party Interventions and the Duration of Intrastate Conflicts." *Journal of Conflict Resolution* 46(1): 55–73. https://doi.org/10.1177/0022002702046001004.

Ryckman, Kirssa Cline, and Alexis Leanna Henshaw. 2025. "Women without a Tactical Advantage: Boko Haram's Female Suicide Bombers." *Conflict Management and Peace Science* [online]. https://doi.org/10.1177/07388942241305235.

Salehyan, Idean. 2010. "The Delegation of War to Rebel Organizations." *Journal of Conflict Resolution* 54(3): 493–515. https://doi.org/10.1177/0022002709357890.

Salehyan, Idean, Kristian Skrede Gleditsch, and David E. Cunningham. 2011. "Explaining External Support for Insurgent Groups." *International Organization* 65(4): 709–44. https://doi.org/10.1017/S0020818311000233.

Salehyan, Idean, David Siroky, and Reed M. Wood. 2014. "External Rebel Sponsorship and Civilian Abuse: A Principal-Agent Analysis of Wartime Atrocities." *International Organization* 68(3): 633–61. https://doi.org/10.1017/S002081831400006X.

San-Akca, Belgin. 2016. *States in Disguise: Causes of State Support for Rebel Groups*. Oxford University Press.

Schultz, Kenneth A. 2001. *Democracy and Coercive Diplomacy*. Cambridge University Press.

Schwarz, Susanne, and Alexander Coppock. 2022. "What Have We Learned About Gender from Candidate Choice Experiments? A Meta-analysis of Sixty-Seven Factorial Survey Experiments." *Journal of Politics* 84(2): 655–68. https://doi.org/10.1086/716290.

Singer, J. David. 1988. "Reconstructing the Correlates of War Dataset on Material Capabilities of States, 1816–1985." *International Interactions* 14(2): 115–32. https://doi.org/10.1080/03050628808434695.

Sivakumaran, Sandesh. 2012. *The Law of Non-international Armed Conflict*. Oxford University Press.

Sixta, Christine. 2008. "The Illusive Third Wave: Are Female Terrorists the New 'New Women' in Developing Societies?" *Journal of Women, Politics and Policy* 29(2): 261–88. https://doi.org/10.1080/15544770802118645.

Sjoberg, Laura. 2013. *Gendering Global Conflict: Toward a Feminist Theory of War*. Columbia University Press.

Sjoberg, Laura. 2018. "Jihadi Brides and Female Volunteers: Reading the Islamic State's War to See Gender and Agency in Conflict Dynamics." *Conflict Management and Peace Science* 35(3): 296–311. https://doi.org/10.1177/0738894217695050.

Sjoberg, Laura, and Caron E. Gentry. 2007. *Mothers, Monsters, Whores: Women's Violence in Global Politics*. Zed Books.

Sjoberg, Laura, Kelly Kadera, and Cameron G. Thies. 2018. "Reevaluating Gender and IR Scholarship: Moving beyond Reiter's Dichotomies toward Effective Synergies." *Journal of Conflict Resolution* 62(4): 848–70. https://doi.org/10.1177/0022002716669207.

Slantchev, Branislav L. 2006. "Politicians, the Media, and Domestic Audience Costs." *International Studies Quarterly* 50(2): 445–77. https://doi.org/10.1111/j.1468-2478.2006.00409.x.

Sputnik International. 2015. "21st Century Amazons: Syrian Army Female Battalion Fights to Defend Syria." December 26. https://sputnikglobe.com/20151226/syria-army-women-soldiers-1032346479.html.

Stack-O'Connor, Alisa. 2007. "Lions, Tigers, and Freedom Birds: How and Why the Liberation Tigers of Tamil Eelam Employs Women." *Terrorism and Political Violence* 19(1): 43–63. https://doi.org/10.1080/09546550601054642.

Stallman, Heidi, and Falak Hadi. 2025. "Gender Inclusion and Rebel Strategy: Legitimacy Seeking Behavior in Rebel Groups." *International Politics* 62(2): 291–317. https://doi.org/10.1057/s41311-024-00561-0.

Stanton, Jessica A. 2016. *Violence and Restraint in Civil War: Civilian Targeting in the Shadow of International Law*. Cambridge University Press. https://doi.org/10.1017/9781107706477.

Stanton, Jessica A. 2020. "Rebel Groups, International Humanitarian Law, and Civil War Outcomes in the Post-Cold War Era." *International Organization* 74(3): 523–59. https://doi.org/10.1017/s0020818320000090.

Stauffer, Katelyn E., and Diana Z. O'Brien. 2018. "Quantitative Methods and Feminist Political Science." In *Oxford Research Encyclopedia of Politics*. https://doi.org/10.1093/acrefore/9780190228637.013.210.

Stewart, Megan A., Jonathan B. Petkun, and Mara R. Revkin. 2024. "The Progressive Case for American Power." *Foreign Affairs*, June 18. www.foreignaffairs.com/united-states/progressive-case-american-power.

Svallfors, Signe. 2024. "Reproductive Justice in the Colombian Armed Conflict." *Disasters* 48(3): 1–22. https://doi.org/10.1111/disa.12618.

Svolik, Milan W. 2012. *The Politics of Authoritarian Rule*. Cambridge University Press.

Szekely, Ora. 2020. "Fighting About Women: Ideologies of Gender in the Syrian Civil War." *Journal of Global Security Studies* 5(3): 408–26. https://doi.org/10.1093/jogss/ogz018 .

Tellander, Ebba, and Cindy Horst. 2019. "A Foreign Policy Actor of Importance? The Role of the Somali Diaspora in Shaping Norwegian

Policy towards Somalia." *Foreign Policy Analysis* 15(1): 136–54. https://doi.org/10.1093/fpa/orx012.

Tessler, Mark, and Ina Warriner. 1997. "Gender, Feminism, and Attitudes toward International Conflict: Exploring Relationships with Survey Data from the Middle East." *World Politics* 49(2): 250–81. https://doi.org/10.1353/wp.1997.0005.

Thomas, Jakana L. 2021. "Wolves in Sheep's Clothing: Assessing the Effect of Gender Norms on the Lethality of Female Suicide Terrorism." *International Organization* 75(3): 769–802. https://doi.org/10.1017/s0020818321000035.

Thomas, Jakana L. 2024. "Sisters Are Doing It for Themselves: How Female Combatants Help Generate Gender-Inclusive Peace Agreements in Civil Wars." *American Political Science Review* 118(2): 831–47. https://doi.org/10.1017/S0003055423000461.

Thomas, Jakana L., and Kanisha D. Bond. 2015. "Women's Participation in Violent Political Organizations." *American Political Science Review* 109(3): 488–506. https://doi.org/10.1017/S0003055415000313.

Thomas, Jakana L., and Reed M. Wood. 2018. "The Social Origins of Female Combatants." *Conflict Management and Peace Science* 35(3): 215–32. https://doi.org/10.1177/0738894217695524.

Toivanen, Mari, and Bahar Baser. 2016. "Gender in the Representations of an Armed Conflict: Female Kurdish Combatants in French and British Media." *Middle East Journal of Culture and Communication* 9(3): 294–314. https://doi.org/10.1163/18739865-00903007.

Tokdemir, Efe, Seden Akcinaroglu, H. Ege Ozen, and Ekrem Karakoc. 2020. "'Wars of Others': National Cleavages and Attitudes towards External Conflicts." *International Interactions* 46(6): 953–86. https://doi.org/10.1080/03050629.2020.1792898.

Tomz, Michael. 2007. "Domestic Audience Costs in International Relations: An Experimental Approach." *International Organization* 61(4): 821–40. https://doi.org/10.1017/S0020818307070282.

Tomz, Michael R., and Jessica L. P. Weeks. 2013. "Public Opinion and the Democratic Peace." *American Political Science Review* 107(4): 849–65. https://doi.org/10.1017/S0003055413000488.

Tomz, Michael R., and Jessica L. P. Weeks. 2020. "Human Rights and Public Support for War." *Journal of Politics* 82(1): 182–94. https://doi.org/10.1086/705741.

Tomz, Michael, Jessica L. P. Weeks, and Keren Yarhi-Milo. 2020. "Public Opinion and Decisions About Military Force in Democracies." *International Organization* 74(1): 119–43. https://doi.org/10.1017/S0020818319000341.

Towns, Ann E. 2010. *Women and States: Norms and Hierarchies in International Society.* Cambridge University Press. https://doi.org/10.1017/CBO9780511779930.

US Central Command [@CENTCOM]. 2017a. "Ready for the Fight." Tweet. *X/Twitter.* https://x.com/CENTCOM/status/836574056468082688.

US Central Command [@CENTCOM]. 2017b. "By Popular Demand, More Photos of the Female Fighters of the Syrian Anti-ISIS Campaign." Tweet. *X/Twitter.* https://x.com/CENTCOM/status/836573860669571072.

US Department of Defense. 2022. "Department of Defense Releases Annual Demographics Report – Upward Trend in Number of Women." US Department of Defense, December 14. www.defense.gov/News/Releases/Release/article/3246268/department-of-defense-releases-annual-demographics-report-upward-trend-in-numbe/.

US Embassy in Tunisia. 2021. "Secretary Barrett and General Harrigian's Visit Demonstrate Tunisia Is a Key Partner." January 8. https://tn.usembassy.gov/secretary-barrett-and-general-harrigians-visit-demonstrate-tunisia-is-a-key-partner/.

Viterna, Jocelyn. 2014. "Radical or Righteous? Using Gender to Shape Public Perceptions." In Lorenzo Bosi, Chares Demetriou, and Stefan Malthaner (eds.), *Dynamics of Political Violence: A Process Oriented Perspective on Radicalization and the Escalation of Political Violence.* Routledge, pp. 189–236.

von Clausewitz, Carl ([1832] 1873). *On War [Vom Krieg],* trans. J. J. Graham. N. Trübner & Co. (A more recent edition is Carl Clausewitz, *On War,* Penguin, 2003.)

Walter, Barbara F. 2015. "Why Bad Governance Leads to Repeat Civil War." *Journal of Conflict Resolution* 59(7): 1242–72. https://doi.org/10.1177/0022002714528006.

Walzer, Michael. 1977. *Just and Unjust Wars.* Basic Books.

Webster, Emma Saran. 2015. "ISIS's Biggest Fear Is Being Killed by Women." *Teen Vogue,* December 14. www.teenvogue.com/story/isis-fear-killed-by-women-heaven.

Weeks, Ana Catalano, Bonnie M. Meguid, Miki Caul Kittilson, and Hilde Coffé. 2023. "When Do Männerparteien Elect Women? Radical Right Populist Parties and Strategic Descriptive Representation." *American Political Science Review* 117(2): 421–38. https://doi.org/10.1017/S0003055422000107.

Weeks, Jessica L. 2008. "Autocratic Audience Costs: Regime Type and Signaling Resolve." *International Organization* 62(1): 35–64. https://doi.org/10.1017/s0020818308080028.

Weeks, Jessica L. 2012. "Strongmen and Straw Men: Authoritarian Regimes and the Initiation of International Conflict." *American Political Science Review* 106(2): 326–47. https://doi.org/10.1017/S0003055412000111.

Weeraratne, Suranjan. 2023. "Why Are Some Suicide Terror Attacks More Newsworthy Than Others?" *Dynamics of Asymmetric Conflict* 16(2): 148–78. https://doi.org/10.1080/17467586.2023.2218900.

Weierstall, Roland, Claudia Patricia Bueno Castellanos, Frank Neuner, and Thomas Elbert. 2013. "Relations among Appetitive Aggression, Post-Traumatic Stress and Motives for Demobilization: A Study in Former Colombian Combatants." *Conflict and Health* 7(1): article 9. https://doi.org/10.1186/1752-1505-7-9.

Weiss, Jessica Chen. 2014. *Powerful Patriots: Nationalist Protest in China's Foreign Relations*. Oxford University Press.

Weiss, Jessica Chen, and Allan Dafoe. 2019. "Authoritarian Audiences, Rhetoric, and Propaganda in International Crises: Evidence from China." *International Studies Quarterly* 63(4): 963–73. https://doi.org/10.1093/isq/sqz059.

Wood, Reed M. 2019. *Female Fighters: Why Rebel Groups Recruit Women for War*. Columbia University Press. https://doi.org/10.7312/wood19298.

Wood, Reed M., and Lindsey Allemang. 2022. "Female Fighters and the Fates of Rebellions: How Mobilizing Women Influences Conflict Duration." *Conflict Management and Peace Science* 39(5): 565–86. https://doi.org/10.1177/07388942211034746.

Wood, Reed M., and Mark D. Ramirez. 2018. "Exploring the Microfoundations of the Gender Equality Peace Hypothesis." *International Studies Review* 20(3): 345–67. https://doi.org/10.1093/isr/vix016.

Wood, Reed M., and Jakana L. Thomas. 2017. "Women on the Frontline: Rebel Group Ideology and Women's Participation in Violent Rebellion." *Journal of Peace Research* 54(1): 31–46. https://doi.org/10.1177/0022343316675025.

Yarhi-Milo, Keren. 2018. *Who Fights for Reputation: The Psychology of Leaders in International Conflict*. Princeton University Press.

Yesiltas, Ozum. 2022. "Understanding Rojava: Representations of Kurdish Women Fighters in US Mainstream Media." *Journal of Middle East Women's Studies* 18(3): 337–58. https://doi.org/10.1215/15525864-10022118.

Yuval-Davis, Nira. 1997. "Women, Citizenship and Difference." *Feminist Review* 57(1): 4–27. https://doi.org/10.1080/014177897339632.

Acknowledgments

Many people have generously offered feedback and support at different stages in the development of this Element, and I am deeply grateful for their engagement. I benefited from thoughtful comments and conversations with Serkant Adiguzel, Olga Avdeyeva, Nuole Chen, Stephen Chaudion, Alexandru Grigorescu, Shana Gadarian, Chris Grady, Alice Iannantuoni, Jeffrey Jensen, Molly Melin, Giuliana Pardelli, John Patty, Jeffrey Timmons, and two anonymous reviewers. Their suggestions helped sharpen both the arguments and the structure of this Element. I also thank the audiences at the 2019 EITM (Empirical Implications of Theoretical Models) Summer Institute, the Gender and Politics Working Group organized by Rachel Bernhard, colleagues at Syracuse University and Sabancı University, and the 2021 APSA (American Political Science Association) Annual Meeting for their valuable feedback on various parts of the manuscript.

I am especially thankful to this series' editors, Tiffany Barnes and Diana O'Brien, for their guidance and encouragement throughout this process. I appreciate your support.

I also want to thank Zeynep Demir and Benan Soydas for their excellent research assistance. Financial support from the Program for the Advancement of Research on Conflict and Collaboration (PARCC) at Syracuse University and the Centennial Center Research Grants of APSA made parts of this research possible – I am grateful for their generous support.

Finally, I am deeply grateful to Ekrem T. Başer. His support – both academic and personal – has been invaluable throughout this process.

Cambridge Elements

Gender and Politics

Tiffany D. Barnes
University of Texas at Austin

Tiffany D. Barnes is Professor of Political Science at the University of Texas at Austin. She is the author of *Women, Politics, and Power: A Global Perspective* (Rowman & Littlefield, 2007) and, award-winning, *Gendering Legislative Behavior* (Cambridge University Press, 2016). Her research has been funded by the National Science Foundation (NSF) and recognized with numerous awards. Barnes is the former president of the Midwest Women's Caucus and founder and director of the Empirical Study of Gender (EGEN) network.

Diana Z. O'Brien
Washington University in St. Louis

Diana Z. O'Brien is the Bela Kornitzer Distinguished Professor of Political Science at Washington University in St. Louis. She specializes in the causes and consequences of women's political representation. Her award-winning research has been supported by the NSF and published in leading political science journals. O'Brien has also served as a Fulbright Visiting Professor, an associate editor at *Politics & Gender*, the president of the Midwest Women's Caucus, and a founding member of the EGEN network.

About the Series

From campaigns and elections to policymaking and political conflict, gender pervades every facet of politics. Elements in Gender and Politics features carefully theorized, empirically rigorous scholarship on gender and politics. The Elements both offer new perspectives on foundational questions in the field and identify and address emerging research areas.

Cambridge Elements

Gender and Politics

Elements in the Series

In Love and at War: Marriage in Non-state Armed Groups
Hilary Matfess

Counter-Stereotypes and Attitudes Toward Gender and LGBTQ Equality
Jae-Hee Jung and Margit Tavits

The Politics of Bathroom Access and Exclusion in the United States
Sara Chatfield

Women, Gender, and Rebel Governance during Civil Wars
Meredith Maloof Loken

Abortion Attitudes and Polarization in the American Electorate
Erin C. Cassese, Heather L. Ondercin and Jordan Randall

Gender, Ethnicity, and Intersectionality in Cabinets: Asia and Europe in Comparative Perspective
Amy H. Liu, Roman Hlatky, Keith Padraic Chew, Eoin L. Power, Sam Selsky, Betty Compton and Meiying Xu

Gendered Jobs and Local Leaders: Women, Work, and the Pipeline to Local Political Office
Rachel Bernhard and Mirya R. Holman

What's Happened to the Gender Gap in Political Activity: Social Structure, Politics, and Participation in the United States Shauna L. Shames, Sara Morell, Ashley Jardina, Kay Lehman Schlozman and Nancy Burns

Family Matters: How Romantic Partners Shape Politicians' Careers
Olle Folke, Moa Frödin Gruneau and Johanna Rickne

Glass Ceilings, Glass Cliffs, and Quicksands: Gendered Party Leadership in Parliamentary Systems
Andrea S. Aldrich and Zeynep Somer-Topcu

Attitudes toward Political Authoritarianism in Economically Advanced Democracies: The Role of Gender Values and Norms
Amy C. Alexander and Gefjon Off

Public Preferences, Gender, and Foreign Support for Armed Movements
Çağlayan Başer

A full series listing is available at: www.cambridge.org/EGAP

For EU product safety concerns, contact us at Calle de José Abascal, 56–1°,
28003 Madrid, Spain or eugpsr@cambridge.org.

www.ingramcontent.com/pod-product-compliance
Lightning Source LLC
LaVergne TN
LVHW011845060526
838200LV00054B/4174